I0411207

United States
Department
of Agriculture

Forest Service

General Technical
Report NC-271

November 2006

Growth and Yield of Red Pine in the Lake States

Robert E. Buckman, Badege Bishaw, T.J. Hanson, and Frank A. Benford

About the Authors:

Robert E. Buckman, Professor (retired), College of Forestry, Oregon State University

Badege Bishaw, Research Associate, College of Forestry, Oregon State University

T.J. Hanson, FEC Consulting, LLC, Beaverton, Oregon

Frank A. Benford, Benford Applied Mathematics, Salem, Oregon

U.S. Department of Agriculture, Forest Service
North Central Research Station
1992 Folwell Avenue
St. Paul, MN 55108
2006
www.ncrs.fs.fed.us

Abstract

Buckman, Robert E.; Bishaw, Badege; Hanson, T.J.; Benford, Frank A. 2006. Growth and yield of red pine in the Lake States. Gen. Tech. Rep. NC-271. St. Paul, MN: U.S. Department of Agriculture, Forest Service, North Central Research Station. 114 p.

This review examines the entire portfolio of active and inactive red pine growth and yield studies maintained by the USDA Forest Service, North Central Research Station and several of its cooperators. The oldest studies date back to the mid-1920s. Available for analysis are 31 experiments and sets of monitoring plots in both planted and natural forests. These contain 3,671 individual growth estimates, 10 times more than previously available. From this dataset is an analysis of stand and tree growth responses and mortality in relation to age, site index, stand density, thinning methods, and other silvicultural factors. A growth and yield model (RP2005) provides a computer-based means to estimate growth and yield and to weigh the consequences of various silvicultural and financial alternatives through time. The analysis then examines the reliability of the prediction model, including comparisons with independent data sets. Appendices describe the database, provide an introduction to RP2005, present the mathematical relationships underlying the model, and define terms.

KEY WORDS: Red pine (*Pinus resinosa* Ait.), Lake States, growth and yield, thinning, thinning methods, spatial characteristics, crown class responses.

Editors Note: PR2005, the computer program related to this manuscript (see Appendix II), is available at the following Web site: http://www.ncrs.fs.fed.us/ library/. Please check this Web site occasionally for corrections or modifications to RP2005, or for other versions of computer program that are likely to evolve through time concerning growth and yield of red pine.

The entire manuscript can be printed, downloaded, or ordered via CD or hard copy at this Web site.

Contents

List of Tables

Preface

Red Pine in the Lake States

Zigmond A. Zasada[1]

My forestry career began in northern Minnesota more than 70 years ago. Several impressions remain from those early days—the waning years of the saw-milling industry, the cut-over and burned-over land, the many then-active small farmsteads and villages, and the hardships of the Depression. But it was also a time for renewal—mobilization of tax-forfeited land into County, State, and National Forests, the Civilian Conservation Corp, improved fire-prevention programs, reforestation efforts, and other widespread and widely accepted improvements in forestry practices.

Red pine even then was central to much of forest conservation in the Lake States. I had the pleasure of knowing some of the pioneers, going back almost to the beginning of the last century, who recognized the potential of red pine, promoted its protection and use, and otherwise did some of the early research on the species. For a number of years following 1939 I was directly involved in developing management guides for Lake States species and in some of the studies described here. In later years I had the opportunity to observe the research of others, and the field practices resulting there from, across all three of the Lake States.

Emerging from this body of information is an evolving pattern of inquiry and field practice that backstops present day red pine silviculture. A key part of this evolution was the establishment and maintenance of long-term permanent sample plots and experiments, the oldest of which used here goes back more than 75 years. While most of the early studies have been replaced by more elaborate experiments, the records of many of them—both active and inactive—are used in this analysis.

A concluding note: At the time of European settlement in the Lake States there were an estimated 22 million acres of red and white pine forests in the Lake States, one-third of which was red pine. Today only about 2 million acres of red pine exist in now hardwood-dominated landscapes, most of it in plantations established since the 1930s. Because white pine, another preferred softwood, is so vulnerable to blister rust, white-pine weevils and animal damage (mainly white-tail deer), red pine remains the softwood of choice for

---

[1] Zigmond A Zasada began his forestry career on the Chippewa National Forest in 1933 and later worked in a variety of research-related jobs in Grand Rapids, Minnesota; Marquette, Michigan; Washington, D.C.; and St. Paul, Minnesota until his retirement from the Forest Service in 1967. He then joined the University of Minnesota at the Cloquet Field Station until he retired again in 1978. In later years he consulted on a number of tasks, including advising the Blandin Foundation on a major red pine reforestation project in Itasca County, Minnesota. He was 94 years old when he wrote this preface, a life-long observer and enthusiast for red pine and for forestry in the Lake States.

reforestation in the Lake States. This monograph makes an important contribution for its management. As the authors recognize, the next generation of research must again address the question of lower cost and more reliable regeneration and reforestation techniques, and how red pine better fits the landscape patterns of the Lake States.

A Note by the Senior Author

Robert E. Buckman

The roots of this work go back to the late 1950s, when three young forestry researchers, myself, Robert Wambach (deceased) and Allen Lundgren, all at the Grand Rapids, Minnesota, Laboratory of the USDA Forest Service, Lake States (now North Central) Forest Experiment Station, collaborated in various ways to better understand the response of red pine to different silvicultural practices and site factors. We, in turn, built on research of others, begun at the turn of the century more than 50 years earlier.

I led off by preparing a variable density growth and yield model for red pine, using 14 sets of experiments and growth plots in both planted and natural stands in Minnesota (Buckman 1962a). The model applied to stands 25 years of age and older.

Shortly thereafter, Wambach examined the behavior of red pine plantations, using data gathered from 55 temporary plots in plantations across Minnesota, Wisconsin, and Michigan (Wambach 1967). His work applied to stands ranging in age from 10 to 35 years.

Lundgren, a contemporary, continued the work for a number of years after Wambach and I moved to other positions. Among his substantial contributions was the linking of young stand growth predictors of Wambach with those in older stands that I had developed (Lundgren 1981). This, in turn, led to a computer-based growth-and-yield model, REDPINE, adopted and modified by others (see page 12 for a further elaboration of the work of these three investigators).

In 1995, Glen Erickson, Forestry Technician at the USDA Forestry Sciences Laboratory in Grand Rapids, Minnesota, invited Lundgren and me to review a manuscript summarizing 45 years of red pine growth information for Plot 99, a small seed source study on the Chippewa National Forest. This plot was of interest because of its lack of genetic variability and its high stand growth rates (fig. 26). We inquired about the status of this and several other studies with which we had been involved up to 40 years earlier. We were told that many had been maintained in all the intervening years and, furthermore, that other long-term red pine studies from Wisconsin and Michigan had been added to the portfolio of the Grand Rapids, Minnesota Laboratory. Except for periodic measurement and treatment of the individual studies, little analytic work had been done on them in the intervening years.

Thus began this reexamination of growth responses of red pine to a variety of thinning and other cultural practices. Essentially, it is an update of earlier efforts to extract information from a now much larger body of information, some of it going back to the inception of red pine studies early in the last century. For me it provided an unusual opportunity and a pleasure to revisit some of the same work that was so interesting and stimulating early in my career.

Joining this effort were Dr. Badege Bishaw, who has spent countless hours editing, summarizing and analyzing the large data base, and Drs. T.J. Hanson and Frank A. Benford, who played key roles, respectively, in creating the computer programs to simulate growth and yield, and in developing the mathematical foundation for the growth functions.

Acknowledgments

Tribute is due the many scientists and professional workers over the years who asked the initial questions about red pine and designed appropriate field experiments to address them, which in turn evolved into additional questions and experiments. Today, nearly a century later, this sequence of questions and experiments provides a foundation for the protection and management of red pine. Many of these visionaries are cited in this paper: for those who are named and those who are not, we are deeply indebted.

Special credit is also due to a dedicated corps of technicians who over the years measured, maintained, and otherwise looked after the many studies used here. Their role was all the more important during periods of inactivity in red pine research. Of note are Lee South (deceased), Clarence Hawkinson (deceased), Robert Barse (retired), and Glen Erickson (retired), who collectively provided more than 60 years of unbroken continuity in maintaining most of the studies used here.

Collaborators who provided land, assisted in maintenance and protection of the various studies, and otherwise generously provided data and counsel include:

- USDA Forest Service: Chippewa, Superior and Huron-Manistee National Forests

- USDA Natural Resources Conservation Service of Michigan

- Minnesota Department of Natural Resources

- Wisconsin Department of Natural Resources and Burnett and Jackson Counties

- Michigan Department of Natural Resources

- Consumers Power Company of Michigan

- Minnesota and Ontario Paper Company (later Boise-Cascade Corp.)

- University of Minnesota, College of Natural Resources

- Michigan State University, Department of Forestry

- Canadian Forestry Service, Petawawa National Forestry Research Institute

- Mr. Sydney Rommel, Grand Rapids, Minnesota

A special thanks to Manuela Huso, who provided mathematical and statistical advice far beyond the capacity of the authors. Other helpful advisors included (in alphabetic order) David H. Alban, Peter Bettinger, Mary Buckman, Kathy Howell, Allen L. Lundgren, Jerry Mohr, Douglas Maguire, D.W. Rose, and George Weaver.

We are most grateful to the following for their constructive criticisms of this manuscript: Robert L. Ethington, Paul D. Anderson, Harold E. Burkhart, Robert O. Curtis, Alan R. Ek, Daniel C. Dey, D.W. Rose, Allen L. Lundgren, Barbara J. Winters, and Robert D. Wray.

The North Central Research Station, the Pacific Northwest Research Station, and the Washington Office, all of the USDA Forest Service, provided financial and logistical support. The College of Forestry, Oregon State University, and the College of Natural Resources, University of Minnesota, also provided technical and logistical support.

Chapter 1. Summary and Conclusions

The earliest silvicultural studies in the Lake States region involved red pine, the most promising conifer to replace the rapidly disappearing white and red pine forests[2] of the 19th and early 20th centuries. The first work addressed forest regeneration, but was followed soon thereafter by formal and informal studies to track red pine growth in relation to a variety of silvicultural treatments on various combinations of stand ages and site qualities.

Examined here are 31 sets of active and inactive experiments and growth-monitoring plots in plantations and natural stands in Minnesota, Wisconsin, and Michigan. These studies are maintained by the USDA North Central Research Station and its cooperators, the oldest dating to the mid-1920s (Appendix I). These contain some 3,671 growth observations representing a wide range of ages (10-190 years), site indices (40-75 ft), and basal area stand densities (30-250+ ft²/acre). Data are of high mensurational quality, but with substantial statistical inadequacies. When compared to independent data from comparable stands, however, growth predictions thus derived appear to be reasonable.

This paper examines red pine stand management practices, including revised growth, yield, and mortality estimates, now with a much larger data base than was previously available.

Stand Age, Site Index, Stand Density, Mortality

Stand age. Growth estimates are projected from the time of stand establishment to age 200+. More rapid growth is observed at young ages (~6-25) than previously recorded, but estimates are less reliable than at older ages. These findings invite a new look at silviculture at young ages, especially where high biomass production is the goal (see stand density on next page).

Site index (SI) and stand height. Over the years site quality has been much studied with generally adequate SI estimating procedures available for red pine. We use a slightly modified version of the Gevorkiantz and Lundgren/Dolid SI curves. Dominant height and stand basal area (BA) are then converted to stand volumes by means of volume equations. For similar thinning regimes, stand yields (standing cubic-foot volume plus accumulated thinnings) more than double from SI 40 to SI 70. SI is one of the most sensitive indicators of stand productivity and economic profitability despite generally higher site preparation and vegetation management costs on better sites.

---

[2] Scientific names are given in Appendix IV.

Stand density. In young stands (ages <20-25) growth is strongly affected by numbers of trees per acre (TPA). Beyond these ages, when sites are fully occupied, TPA has little predictive value for stand growth. BA, rather than TPA, becomes the more useful expression of stand density. Beyond ~age 25, BA growth is approximately equal over a wide range (~90-200 ft²/acre) of BA densities. Cubic volume growth, however, increases with higher stand densities, more so on better sites and at younger ages, when height growth is most rapid. Individual tree growth (as contrasted to stand growth), however, is strongly affected by tree numbers and BA at all ages.

Height growth of the dominant stand is unaffected over the wide range of stand densities commonly used in red pine management. Prompt and successful establishment of new stands, and aggressive release from competing vegetation (i.e., aspen, birch, oaks, hazel, grasses and forbs), greatly favors red pine growth and weighs strongly and positively in economic analysis.

Stand mortality. Some 907 plot observations, about 25 percent of total stands, experienced endemic BA mortality ranging from near-zero to about 5 ft²/acre/yr. Overall mortality (excluding catastrophic losses) averaged about 3.4 percent of gross basal area growth. This was somewhat greater in high-density and older stands, otherwise substantially lower than average in younger and lower density stands. Catastrophic mortality (as contrasted to endemic mortality) is difficult to estimate, but fire and wind vulnerability, animal damage, and excessive stand density (beyond say 200 ft²/acre) should be anticipated during the layout and management of stands in order to reduce risk.

Wood quality. Silviculture affects such wood quality attributes as radial growth rates, size of individual trees, branch and crown sizes (hence knot characteristics and stem taper), and to some extent specific gravity and size of juvenile cores. Our ability to predict these consequences is limited. Perhaps the greatest opportunity to improve overall wood quality, however, comes from early thinning that removes defective, diseased, and malformed trees and species of lesser value, shifting growth to higher-quality red pine stems.

Thinning Methods, Crown Classes, Spatial Arrangements

Thinning methods (above, below, combination). Up to mid-range BA densities (<120 ft²/acre) stands thinned-from-above consistently outgrow (but with considerable variability) those thinned-from-below. These responses are even more pronounced at low densities than at mid-range (table 1). Little growth difference is found among thinning methods at densities >120 ft²/acre. Repeated thinning from above reduces dominant height (~2-5 ft) but with small consequences for stand growth. Thinning methods offer substantial tradeoffs in size of trees harvested and those remaining, affording many silvicultural and economic options now and in the future (table 2).

Crown class responses. Up to mid-range initial stand densities (<120 ft²/acre), intermediate and smaller codominant trees capture a larger share of stand growth than do dominant trees. At mid-range densities (~120-150 ft²/acre) growth is distributed approximately equally among crown classes. Above ~150 ft²/acre (including unthinned stands) growth shifts toward dominant crown classes, with smaller classes falling behind and eventually dying (figs. 22-24). The two approaches to stand structure analysis—thinning methods and crown classes—exhibit remarkable consistency in explaining stand-structure growth responses. RP2005 permits estimating quadratic mean diameter (QMD) changes associated with stand structure manipulation.

Spatial relationships. For stands of similar residual densities, no differences were found in long-term growth rates between uniformly spaced and row-thinned stands. Similarly, for stands of comparable residual densities, intensity of thinning (removal of up to 2/3 of a stand BA in a single thinning) has little impact on future growth. Variability of tree diameters (presumably an indicator of uniform tree spacing) has no predictive value for stand growth. Evidence suggests that below-ground conditions (wide-spreading and intertwined root systems, symbiotic fungi, root grafts) better explain many growth responses to thinning than do crown conditions.

Growth forecasting. RP2005, based on newly developed growth equations (Appendix II and III), allows the user to simulate growth, yield, and mortality for a variety of products and tree sizes in both natural and planted stands. The model also permits financial analysis of silvicultural and managerial options. This growth model, when tested against independent sets drawn from comparable red pine populations, provides reasonably consistent results

Skilled users can build new or revised models (generally with a new name) by modifying or otherwise substituting other program languages to describe the production response information shown in the text and Appendix III.

Next Generation

Unfinished business. Included are development of reliable techniques for natural regeneration of existing stands; restoration of pine to former sites (especially on better quality land); consequences of conifer restoration on now-hardwood-dominated landscapes; better quantitative growth estimators to describe cutting methods and crown class responses; improved estimates of growth in young ages (~ages 5-25); marketing studies aimed at better utilization of the rapidly increasing supply of red pine timber; and a better understanding of below-ground growth processes.

Chapter 2. Introduction, Silviculture, Historical Perspective

"Norway pine, or red pine as it is sometimes called, is a tree whose importance is certain to increase". Woolsey and Chapman 1914.

Introduction and Objectives

Red pine has been examined longer and more intensively than any other tree species in the Lake States because it was among the most promising conifers (along with eastern white pine) for the generation of forests following the extensive logging and forest fires of the 19th and early 20th centuries. Today red pine, because of its high volume growth rates, relative freedom from insect and disease damage, and low mortality, is the preferred conifer for reforestation. Early and sustained interest in red pine was aimed primarily at timber production. In more recent years, especially on public land, has come a growing appreciation of the ecological, recreational, and aesthetic values of the remnants of natural forests and of older plantations—and the practices required to enhance those values. Some of the information developed here will relate to non-timber as well as timber values.

Over the decades that followed the original logging, a series of observations and increasingly sophisticated experiments evolved to examine silvicultural options for stand management. This report is another in a nearly century-long series of summaries of red pine stand management, each with more information and more powerful analytic tools than its predecessor.

The objectives of this study are to:

- Review briefly the historical aspects of research related to red pine stand management.
- Better understand the silvicultural options available to users in light of a greatly expanded dataset and knowledge base.
- Develop growth and mortality equations based on the expanded dataset.
- Incorporate these new equations into a growth and yield model (RP2005) to track the consequences of various silvicultural and economic alternatives in relation to age, SI, and stand density.
- Test the model against independent data sets and otherwise explore the risks and uncertainties that surround red pine management.

The intended audiences for the main body of the text are land managers and field foresters—those responsible for the long-term management and protection of red pine forests and those who perform the day-to-day tasks to achieve the goals and objectives derived there from. We use English (or Imperial) units of measure since they remain the working language of this group (See Appendix IV for metric equivalents, definitions of terms, and scientific names).

In the main body of the text, we strive to develop an understanding of red pine growth behavior in relation to a variety of silvicultural and managerial options. Here we use relatively few mathematical terms, relying instead on description and tabular and graphic displays to illustrate key points.

In Appendix I we lay out the extent, purpose, and protocols behind our extensive dataset, which includes both planted and natural stands.

In Appendix II we introduce RP2005, the most recent in a series of computer programs that allows the user to simulate growth and yield of even-aged red pine stands in relation to a number of stand variables and management options. RP2005 contains sidebar instructions and a Users Manual to assist in its application.

Appendix III elaborates on the mathematical background of equation development for those who wish to dig deeper or otherwise modify or substitute the underlying Excel program.

The analysis is primarily at the stand level (as contrasted to tree level), although we develop equations to characterize average stand diameter changes associated with various silvicultural alternatives. As in our earlier work, growth in relation to stand age, site quality, and stand density (and now stand mortality) remains the principal focus. Here, because of the larger database, we substantially extend the range and reliability of estimates for each of these growth factors. In addition, we examine several other variables of silvicultural and economic importance, including thinning methods, crown class responses, row thinning, tree spacing variability, numbers of trees per acre, and thinning intensity.

In terms of new findings, this analysis adds emphasis to the importance of growth behavior in very young stands (say up to age 25~30), and the opportunities to manipulate stand structure by thinning methods in order to achieve a variety of management goals.

At several points we call attention to options that might enhance the consequences of one or another management practice. It is not our intent to set either explicit or implicit goals for red pine management. Instead, we provide information that permits one to weigh the outcome of any one of several pathways (with the assistance of RP2005) toward owner/manager specified goals.

Where appropriate in the main body of the text, we provide brief statistical descriptors to estimate the reliability of relationships among variables. We explore the question of reliability and uncertainty, including comparisons with independent datasets in Chapter 10. Finally, we would like to acknowledge that our forecasting procedures are more sensitive as diagnostic tools (e.g., what stand density to strive for, how many trees to plant, and effects of age and site quality on stand growth) than they are for estimating growth responses on large and variable stands of red pine. Even here, however, we touch on the question of adjusting for growth projections on large and non-uniform red pine stands.

Ecology and Silviculture

In the mid-19th century red pine made up about a third of the 22 million acres of red and white pine forests of the Lake States, much of it in mature and old-growth forests. But by the early 20th century, following massive logging, conversion of some land to agriculture and other non-forest uses, and losses from extensive wildfires, red pine was reduced to about 0.6 percent of the forestland of the Lake States, or about 300,000 acres.

Today red pine occupies nearly 2 million acres of timberland, still only about 4 percent of the commercial forestland of the three states, with most of the increase in plantations. Current net growth rates across the Lake States averages about 80 ft³/acre/yr (Schmidt 2002), a rate likely to increase as recently established stands advance in age (fig. 1).

In some localities, red pine suffers losses from animal, insect, and disease damage, but less so than other tree species. It is moderately resistant to wind, ice, and snow damage, and exhibits little genetic variability across its natural range. It is shade-intolerant, thus grows in even-aged stands, often in mixture with other even-aged conifers and hardwoods. Once established, it requires minimal tending except for early release from competing vegetation (mainly shrubs and broad-leaved trees), protection from catastrophic wildfires, and periodic thinning. The silviculture and ecology of red pine is further summarized by Benzie (1977), Benzie and McCumber (1983), and Rudolf (1990).

Figure 1. *A 240-year-old red pine stand in Itasca State Park, Minnesota. Red pine grows in stand-like conditions for 250 or more years, and individual trees may live beyond 400 years. (Photo—R. Buckman).*

Let us touch on the question of red pine productivity. In side-by-side comparisons of stand growth, red pine almost always fared better than jack pine, aspen, white spruce, and northern hardwoods, often substantially so (Schlaegel 1975; Stone 1976; Frederick and Coffman 1978; Alban 1978, 1985). Among conifers, only eastern white pine on good sites, (when relatively free of white pine weevil and white pine blister rust), can grow as fast or faster than red pine (Anderson et al. 2002). On some sites, cottonwoods and hybrid poplars may exceed red pine volume growth as well.

In a yield comparison with important conifers in the southeastern U.S., Lundgren (1982, 1983), using then existing growth functions for managed stands on medium sites, compared volume production of two 30-year rotations of loblolly and slash pine with one 60-year rotation of red pine. Individual trees of the two southern pines grew faster both in height and diameter, but over 60 years the cumulative stand volume of one rotation of red pine was slightly higher than two 30-year rotations of loblolly pine and considerably higher than two rotations of slash pine. Douglas-fir on medium sites, with its early and sustained diameter and height growth, can outpace red pine by about 20 percent over those same 60 years (Lundgren unpublished).

Red pine productivity compared to other important conifers in the U.S. is high, but visually deceptive. Red pine is a slow starter, relatively short in stand stature, and late to achieve large stem diameters, all of which weigh against red pine in financial analyses. Despite these apparent disadvantages, red pine performs better at higher stand densities than many conifers; grows rapidly in basal area, reaches culmination of MAI later (50-70 years or later depending on thinning regime, SI, and product specification); maintains reasonably high volume growth rates out to ages 150-200 years; and has low mortality.

Red pine is or can be used for almost any product made from conifers—lumber, pulpwood and paper, fence posts, railroad ties, poles, round timber piles, cabin logs, plywood, and structural flakeboard (see Chapter 6 on wood quality). Its wood properties are similar to ponderosa pine (Bowyer 2002), and it takes wood preservatives well. As we will show, there are opportunities to manipulate stand density and structure, both in the short- and long-term, to enhance the production of these products. Today only about one-fifth of the annual growth of red pine is harvested (Schmidt 2002), in part because many stands are still in small size classes, and in part because markets are inadequately developed.

Two areas of silvicultural and ecological research invite further inquiry, both beyond the scope of this study. The first is to develop a reliable means of natural regeneration—to recreate or approximate the natural processes that maintained the red and white pine forests of northeastern U.S. and southeastern Canada in the pre-European settlement era. Since red pine is one of the most fire dependent pines of the world, this will almost certainly involve the use of summer or early autumn forest fires—those that consume large surface fuels and the humus layers that otherwise provide unfavorable seed beds and a haven for competing vegetation. None of the alternatives (mechanical site preparation, light surface fires, or herbicides) creates adequate conditions, especially on medium and better sites, to assure reliable natural regeneration. As a side note, we should point out that those who want to establish new forests promptly will continue to plant cutover or otherwise disturbed forestland. But where natural ecological processes are preferred, as on some public land, reliable natural regeneration remains a desirable but elusive alternative.

The second is to reach beyond stand studies to better understand the landscape influences of red pine (and other conifers) on wildlife, aesthetics, and other natural resources. This line of inquiry promises to enhance biological diversity across the broad reaches of the Lake States, landscapes now dominated by hardwoods.

Historical Perspective

We used 31 sets of data, those from the USDA Forest Service North Central Station and their collaborators, for this work. The datasets are described in Appendix I. Over the years additional studies were also undertaken by several state forestry agencies and Universities and in southeastern Canada by the Canadian Forestry Service and the Province of Ontario. Where appropriate we have referred to these studies in the text and have used several of them for independent tests of growth estimates (fig. 2).

Figure 2. *Bena Plots 1-4 at stand age 125. This study, now retired, represents the oldest data used in this analysis, with measurements beginning in 1925. It was intended as a natural regeneration trial (largely unsuccessful), but overstory growth was followed for nearly 50 years. It is one of three old-growth stands used in this analysis (Photo—R. Buckman).*

Pre-World War II

Shortly after the Civil War (1861-1865) came a growing apprehension about the well-being of American forests. Many of these concerns focused on the Lake States, then the center of U.S. timber production from its white and red pine forests. The earliest silvicultural work, understandably, addressed questions of forest regeneration. The Morris Act of 1902, for example, required that 5 percent of the standing volume of pines (increased to 10 percent in 1908) remain as seed trees on what is now the Chippewa National Forest. The regeneration aspects of this extensive trial, involving mainly red pine, was mostly a failure (Chapman 1946, Eyre and Zehngraff 1948). However, this led to still other experiments in the regeneration of red pine (also largely failures), in which overstory growth was carefully measured, thus providing data for this study.

Plantation forestry as an alternative to natural regeneration also had its start early in the 20th century. In addition to the Chapman Plantation (fig. 3), other red pine plantations were established in the Lake States beginning about 1910. Long-term thinning experiments were later installed in several of them (including Bosom Field , Buck Creek, Croton Dam, Ravenna, and Sooner Club studies in Michigan, and Birch Lake and Plot 99 studies in Minnesota), and they provide many of the data used in this analysis. Other pre-WWII plantations have thinning studies maintained by collaborators in all three Lake States and Canada and provide key sources of information for assessing our growth models against independent data sources.

By the mid-1920s, interest broadened from regeneration to involve intermediate stand management practices in natural stands, including pre-commercial and commercial thinning. Two such studies used here are the "Graveyard" and "Common Sense" plots on the Chippewa National Forest. These studies provided 25 years or more of stand response information, to be replaced by more comprehensive studies following WWII. The 1930s saw the advent of the Civilian Conservation Corp and other depression-era programs that greatly enhanced public forestry in the Lake States. Much of what had been learned from existing red pine research—tree nursery and planting techniques, pre-commercial and commercial thinning, release from competing vegetation, and pruning—was applied.

Little red pine research was begun during WWII, except that monitoring plots were installed in two old-growth stands, Marcell plots 1-14 in 1944 and Lake 13 plots 1-11 in 1945, both on the Chippewa National Forest. These studies are still active. These, plus the now-terminated Bena plots, provide the only information in this study for old-growth stands. Despite their limitations, these data are indispensable for characterizing the growth of stands at advanced ages.

Summaries of early red pine research and development were prepared by Woolsey and Chapman (1914) and Eyre and Zehngraff (1948).

Figure 3. *The Chapman plantation at the University of Minnesota North Central Research and Outreach Center near Grand Rapids, Minnesota, one of the oldest red pine plantations (1901/02) in the Lake States. H.H. Chapman, then Superintendent of the Experiment Station, later Professor of Forestry at Yale University, was a pioneer in red pine management. Some of the growth data used here (from 1930 onward) come from this plantation. (Photo—R. Buckman).*

Post-WWII

Shortly after WWII and continuing into the early 1960s came strengthened forestry research and a reexamination of the red pine studies of the Lake States (now North Central) Forest Experiment Station. Statistically designed thinning experiments, with broadly contrasting treatments, replaced earlier unreplicated studies in both planted and natural stands (fig. 4). Treatments included an array of BA density studies in intermediate-aged stands, plantation tree-spacing experiments, thinning methods (above, below, above-and-below), row thinning, and a cutting cycles study (terminated after 6 years because stand density studies provided essentially the same information).

Several studies included unthinned treatments, which enhanced an understanding of tree and stand behavior at high densities. Fourteen of the studies (both pre- and post-WWII) are in natural stands, all in Minnesota. The remainder are in planted forests in the other two Lake States. And several datasets originated as growth monitoring plots rather

Figure 4. *The Cutfoot stand density study at age 90. Originally a mixed red and jack pine forest following forest fire about 1870, this stand has been monitored continuously by thinning studies since 1927. Now 130 years of age, portions of the stand have been thinned as many as 10 times (Photo—R. Buckman).*

than statistically designed studies. A number of post WWII studies were terminated after 30 years or so of repeated measurement and treatment. Most, however, continue today, providing nearly 45 years of repeated measurement and treatment.

Similar red pine studies, most in planted forests, were begun, among others, by Fred Wilson of the Wisconsin Department of Natural Resources; Maurice Day and Victor Rudolph of Michigan State University; J.H. Allison and T. Schantz-Hansen of the University of Minnesota; and Will Stiell, A.B. Berry, and others in Canada. Many of these studies reinforce and otherwise provide an independent source of information for this study.

Hundreds of papers have originated over the years from these many studies. We cite a number of them as we examine individual aspects of red pine growth and yield.

Early in the post-WWII period, Buckman (1962a) characterized net annual growth of red pine stands over a wide range of densities and ages, and to a lesser extent with respect to SI, using then-available growth information in Minnesota. He fitted a mathematical function to periodic BA increment on 235 sample plots with 324 measurement periods, and used the resulting equations to develop BA and stand volume output tables for a range of ages, stand densities and sites. They were the first of this type of variable density yield tables available for red pine and among the earliest efforts to develop compatible growth and yield models for even-aged species. Although Buckman was limited by the capabilities of computers at that time to simple quadratic equations, the resulting BA growth equation is still in use.

Wambach (1967) studied the development of planted red pine stands, using information collected from 55 temporary plots on different site qualities and tree spacings across the Lake States. The equation fitted to his data provided an estimate of future BA in stands up to ages 25-30, starting with a specified number of established trees (~5 years following planting) per acre. He also investigated the influence of initial spacing on such quality factors as specific gravity and the number and size of branches. His work had an immediate and significant impact on reducing red pine plantation densities in the Lake States.

Lundgren (1981) continued the red pine work for several years after Wambach's and Buckman's careers moved in other directions. Among his contributions was the merging of the young stand equations developed by Wambach with the older stand equations prepared by Buckman. From this he developed the growth and yield simulation model REDPINE (Lundgren 1985), which, with the rapidly growing capacity of computers, could simulate a wide range of management alternatives. These, at least in part, provided a foundation for others to explore silvicultural, economic, and managerial options available for red pine.

In many respects, the work of Buckman, Wambach, and Lundgren sets the stage 40 years later for a revisit to growth and yield of red pine in the Lake States.

Chapter 3. Factors Affecting Growth

In this section we examine stand growth in relation to age, site, and stand density. Two factors—stand age and site quality—have been traditional growth predictors for even-aged stands since the inception of normal yield tables in the 19th century. Stand density as the third variable came into play in the years following WWII. Information from studies such as those used here, combined with the rapidly increasing analytic power of computers, made it possible to study these variables in ever greater detail and sophistication.

We look at each of the three variables in this order: stand age, site quality, and stand density, recognizing that they are greatly interdependent. These relationships become increasingly complex with the addition of each variable, especially so for stand density. In this chapter, we emphasize basal area (BA) and height behavior of stands, deferring exploration of mortality, tree diameter, and volume growth to following sections. All of this leads to the creation of a growth and yield forecasting model (RP2005), developed from the 3,671 growth observations in our datasets.

Of the three variables, age-related responses were difficult to describe up to about age 25, but simpler thereafter. To avoid confusion, we use *age-from-seed* throughout to characterize the age of both planted and natural stands.

Site quality (and site index) relationships, have historically been examined independently of other silvicultural questions. They are treated separately here as well. Later, stand height is merged with BA (in Chapter 9, on volume growth and in the growth model RP2005) to estimate cubic-foot and board-foot stand volumes.

The third variable, stand density, is characterized in two ways. For younger stands, density is described by numbers of trees per acre (TPA). For stands 20-30 years and older, it is measured in BA (ft^2/acre). We then merge the two measures of density, with overlap in the age range of ~15-30, where either can be used.

The reader should keep in mind that BA and TPA play central roles in other ways in this analysis. Stand BA and TPA, for example, are essential for determining quadratic mean tree diameters (QMD) through time, thus RP2005 requires both measures at all stand ages. In addition, our growth model uses BA as the primary response (or dependent) variable, which in turn offers advantages in the numerical summation of growth increments and the conversion of these (combined with dominant stand height) into stand volumes. Also, so convenient is BA that we often characterize growth responses in terms of BA rather than volume. We recognize that users will be far more interested in volume than BA, so, as appropriate, we attempt to reconcile the relationships between the two measures.

We should note that over the years, stand density, as a descriptor of site occupancy, has invited much inquiry in its own right (e.g., Curtis 1970) for many tree species including red pine. For red pine, BA and TPA have become the most commonly used measures of stand density, both for field application and for scientific work. When combined with other stand variables such as age and SI, they are highly useful predictors of stand behavior.

Stand Age

Figure 5 displays periodic annual increment (PAI) in BA (gross ft²/acre/year) growth against stand age and SI for the 3,671 plot observations used in this study. The SI curves assume a BA density of 123 ft²/acre, the average for the 3,671 observations. If one wished, other age/BA/SI relationships could be constructed. Let us examine, first, the BA growth aspects of this display, and shortly in figure 6, those for cubic-foot growth.

Figure 5. *Gross stand BA growth (PAI in ft²/acre/yr) in relation to stand age and SI for the 3,671 observations used in this study. The superimposed SI curves assume a BA of 123 ft²/acre, the average stand density for all observations.*

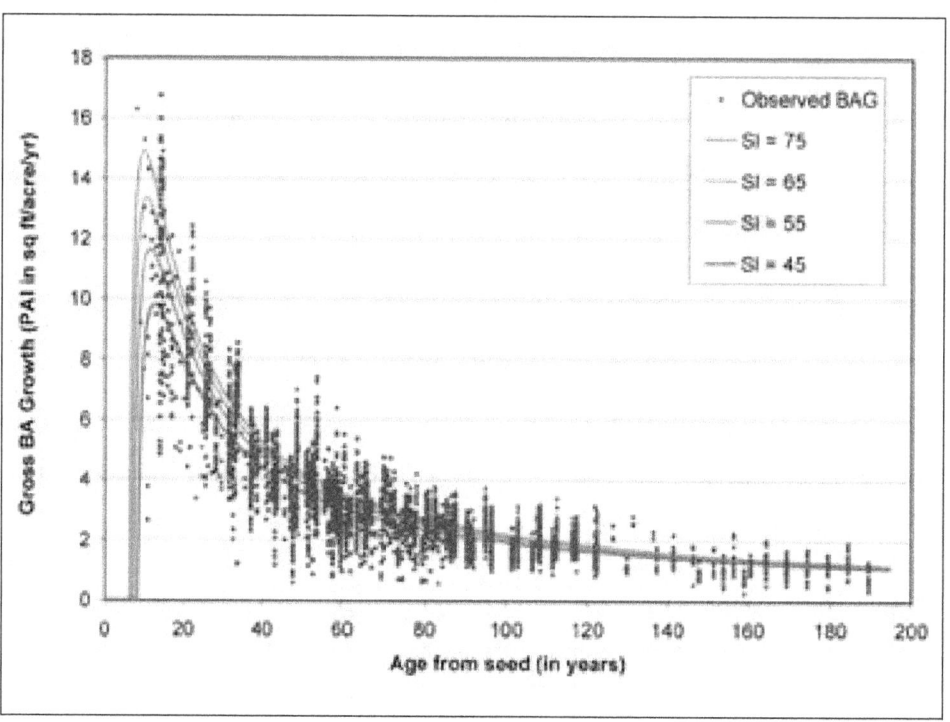

Several points to note about BA growth in relation to stand age:

- PAI declines steadily and predictably from approximately ages 15-25 out to age 200 or more. Some of the scatter of observations surrounding the trend lines can be accounted for by variation in SI and BA density, but some random variation remains.

- Most observations are in the 30- to 100-year age range, reflecting the historical emphasis on thinning studies in already merchantable stands. Most information in this age range is derived from better designed thinning studies than found in older age groups, and undergrids inferences about the effects of stand density and SI in these older age classes (for which data are not nearly so abundant).

- BA PAI grows rapidly from about the ages 6-9 when trees reach breast height (4.5 ft), which we call "breakout age," to a culmination at ages 15-25 or thereabouts. Notice the relatively few observations and their large scatter at these young ages. So dynamic is growth in this age range and so important is it to later stand development that it deserves much more attention in future studies.

- BA mortality through time is not shown in this figure. BA mortality is minimal at young ages and at low- and mid-range stand densities, somewhat higher at ages >150 years and at BA densities >200 ft^2/acre (see Chapter 4).

Cubic-foot volume growth (PAI in ft^3/acre/year) is shown in figure 6. Several observations about stand volume growth in relation to age include the following:

- High growth rates are maintained on better sites in the 20-80 year range, and surprisingly respectable growth rates continue out to ages approaching 200 years. These volume growth rates generally exceed those of other managed even-aged species in the Lake States and compare favorably with some important pine species elsewhere in the U.S.

- Cubic-foot volume growth culminates 10-15 years later than does BA growth. This occurs because the fastest stand height growth lags several years behind the fastest BA growth. Since volume is made up of both the BA and height, maximum cubic-volume PAI is shifted to later ages.

- In contrast to the BA display (fig. 5), notice the greater spread in individual observations (and the SI curves derived there from) because the height of stands so strongly influences volume and volume growth.

We say little more about stand age at this point. It is the indispensable mile marker in the silviculture of even-aged stands. We believe that we have captured this dimension of growth reasonably well, especially for growth in stand ages >20-30.

Figure 6. *Gross cubic foot-volume stand growth (PAI ft³/acre/year) in relation to stand age and SI for the 3,671 observations used in this study. The SI curves assume a stand density of 123 ft²/acre, the average density for all data.*

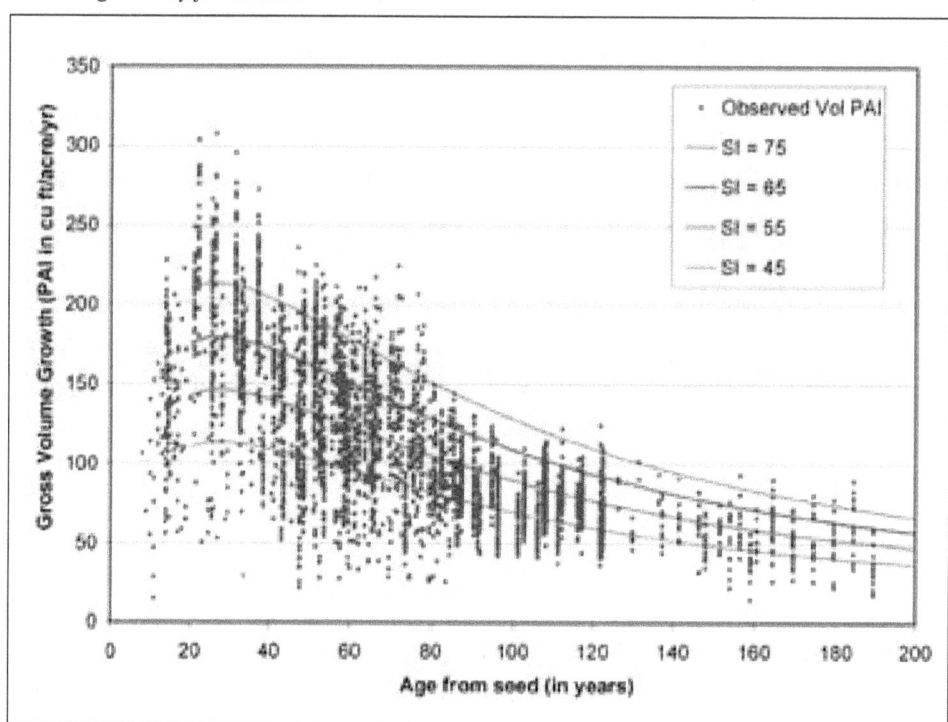

Site Quality, Site Index, and Height Growth

Site quality, the relative ability of forestland to produce biomass, has received as much attention for red pine as it has for many other tree species. Several methods have been tested to estimate site productivity, including soil characteristics, indicator plants, and height of dominant trees in a stand. Alban (1984) and Carmean and Thrower (1995) among others have reviewed questions of red pine site productivity.

Estimating Site Index

We use site index (SI, mean height of dominant and codominant trees at age 50) as a measure of productivity for two reasons: (1) SI has proven a reliable quantitative indicator of stand productivity, and (2) SI provides a means by which average dominant stand height can be estimated at any age.

Red pine SI relationships used here were originally developed from unpublished data gathered in 1916 by H.H. Richmond in northern Minnesota, and later published by Gevorkiantz (1957). They were extended to younger and older ages and reduced to equations by Lundgren and Dolid (1970). These equations were slightly modified and extended by Benford (Appendix III) to pass exactly through the index height at age 50, and to more realistically reflect slower height growth from age 0 to 20. These modifications, embodied in figure 7 below, are of such small practical consequence for stands 20 years and older that the Gevorkiantz graphs, the Lundgren/Dolid equations, and the slightly modified equations developed here can be used interchangeably.

Figure 7. *Site curves (index age 50) for red pine. Plotted points represent the range of the original Richmond/Gevorkiantz data; curves beyond those points portray extensions and modifications by Lundgren/Dolid and Benford.*

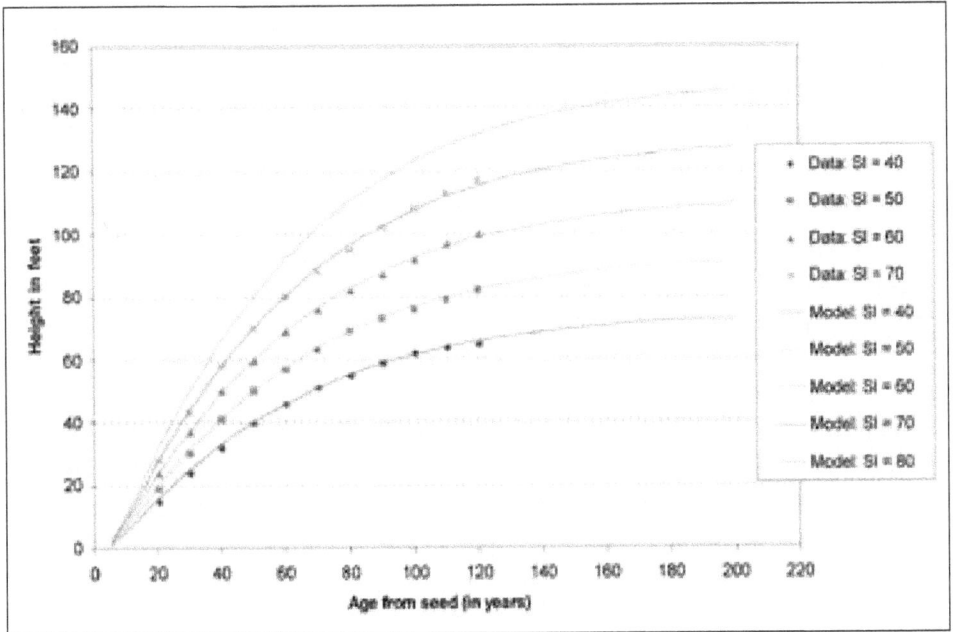

The SI relationships derived from the original H.H. Richmond data have often been challenged. And yet they survive across broad reaches of the Lake States because they track red pine height growth surprisingly well (Alban and Prettyman 1984, Alban 1984, Lundgren unpublished)

For both planted and natural stands it is virtually certain for a variety of reasons (faulty planting practices, competing vegetation at young and intermediate ages, soil and water table variations) that individual stands and groups of stands in localized areas will depart from the stand height patterns shown in figure 7. Where this occurs, several corrective steps are possible. Stand age could be adjusted if there are lags in early height growth, or one could use the volume adjustment procedure available in RP2005 to reflect reduced or delayed height stand growth. If other height growth functions better represent local conditions, the computer program RP2005 could be modified.

Height estimates for all data sets were obtained from five to eight sample trees on each plot. If the plot had been repeatedly measured through time, we used the most recent height estimates. Where crown classes were recorded, dominant and codominant heights were averaged. Where they were not, the tallest 75 percent of the trees were assumed to be dominants and codominants. These height estimates, combined with stand age, were entered in the Lundgren/Dolid equation to estimate SI.

Site determination for the 55 Wambach temporary sample plots used the same underlying SI curves as above. However, Wambach and other investigators (Alban 1979, Bottenfield and Reed 1988, and others) used the 5-year growth intercept method rather than total height to estimate SI in these young stands.

SI estimation presented three statistical and analytic problems. First, it is statistically significant in our growth equations, but is not as strongly correlated with BA or BA growth as are age and stand density. This manifests itself when one commonly observes densities of 200 ft²/acre or more of BA in fully stocked unthinned stands on poor sites, and rarely more than 250-300 ft² on the best sites.

The second problem relates to the age at which trees attain breast height (which we call "breakout age") on various sites. Our data at these young ages were too limited and variable to address this issue adequately. However, a number of investigators have asked similar questions in conjunction with survival and release studies in young red pine stands (Day et al. 1960, Alban and Prettyman 1984, Carmean and Thrower 1995, Lundgren unpublished). These studies reflect the variability in the time it takes for trees to reach breast height age, which ranges from about 5 years (from seed) on best sites to 11 years on poor sites. For this analysis we assume about 6 years for the best sites and 9 years for the poorest sites (Appendix III, figure 29). These ages presume that trees, whether planted or natural, are relatively free of competition from other vegetation, insect and disease infestations, or animal damage, and thus represent the most favorable conditions for young stand growth.

The third problem concerns sampling inadequacies for SI. The individual observations in each of the 31 data sets represent highly correlated estimates of SI. Furthermore, all observations for SI in stands older than 100 years came from only four studies, all on average sites (SI 45-60) in natural stands on the Chippewa National Forest in Minnesota.

Importance of Site Quality

When the height dimension of stand growth (as contrasted with BA) is considered, SI becomes important indeed. Using identical thinning regimes, MAI (ft³/acre/year) volume growth may be more than twice as much on SI 70 than on SI 40 land (figure 6 and Chapter 9). Off-setting increased productivity are the generally higher stand establishment and management costs of better sites, due largely to control of competing vegetation (fig. 8). Nevertheless, site quality invariably turns out to be one of the most sensitive management factors to consider when weighing investment opportunities in red pine. RP2005 provides a means to weigh these and other economic questions.

Figure 8. *Seed-trees on high site (SI ~70) land in Minnesota. The earliest red pine research in the Lake States was aimed at natural regeneration, which was and continues to be largely unsuccessful, especially on better sites. A major challenge on these sites is to develop more reliable and lower-cost techniques to naturally or artificially regenerate existing stands and to reclaim land once occupied by red and white pine (Photo—R. Buckman).*

Stand Establishment and Weed Control

The importance of sound stand establishment practices needs to be underscored. While not a formal part of this analysis, field experience and red pine literature affirm many times over the value of good site preparation, quality and care of planting stock, and early and complete release from competing herbaceous and woody vegetation (i.e., Benzie 1977, Gunter and Rudolph 1968, Buckman and Lundgren 1962, Stone 1976, and many others). There is no doubt that some of our difficulties in characterizing young stand growth stems from these sources of variability.

Without exception, delays in establishing vigorous stands weigh heavily and negatively on investment payoffs for red pine. Indeed, aggressive stand establishment probably counts more in overall red pine productivity than do refinements in many of the individual stand practices described later.

As we pointed out earlier, an important assumption is that planted and natural stands follow similar height/age growth patterns, a premise that remains workable but needs more testing and refinement. On favorable and competition-free sites (for example old fields), planted stands generally get off to a fast start (fig. 9). This, in turn, creates an apparent SI increase that may or may not carry through the life of the stand. Similarly, especially in natural stands with under- or overstory competition, early height growth may be retarded, creating an apparent depression in SI. If height growth is retarded early in the life of a stand, one may wish to adjust ages or insert a correction factor in RP2005 (See section on estimating site index, p. 18)

Figure 9. *Old-field planting sites represent the largely competition-free environments needed to assure prompt and uniform stand growth. Where competing vegetation is present, its early and sustained control is among the most profitable investments in red pine silviculture.*

Stand Density

Stand density, the third variable in this analysis, adds greatly to the complexity of growth forecasting. Especially challenging are the differences in BA growth behavior between young (say up to ages 15-30) and older stands. Adding to this complexity, in field practice the number of established TPA in young stands is the more convenient measure of density, while in older stands BA is more useful.

Growth Behavior—Young Stands

Let us illustrate these points with examples from two well-designed, long-term experiments—for younger stands, the Spooner Plantation Spacing study in Burnette County in Northwestern Wisconsin, and for older stands, the Birch Lake Plantation Density/Thinning Methods Study near Ely, Minnesota.

First, young stands. Figure 10 displays the 40-year gross BA development of un-thinned-spacing plots in the Spooner study. All spacings (in feet) attain breast height at about age 7 on this SI 65-70 land. At age 20, when first measurements were made, the 5x5 spacing had accumulated nearly twice the BA as the 11x11 spacing, with the 7x7 and 9x9 spacings intermediate. Beyond age 20, however, the trend lines are nearly parallel, indicating in this age range that BA growth is approximately equal for all spacings. The explanation for this growth behavior is straight forward. Up to about age 20, larger numbers of trees occupy the site quickly, thus accumulating BA faster. At about age 20, the site approaches full occupancy after which TPA has far less influence on stand growth.

Figure 10. *Spooner plantation spacing study showing gross BA development in unthinned stands in relation to age and spacing (SI ~65-70).*

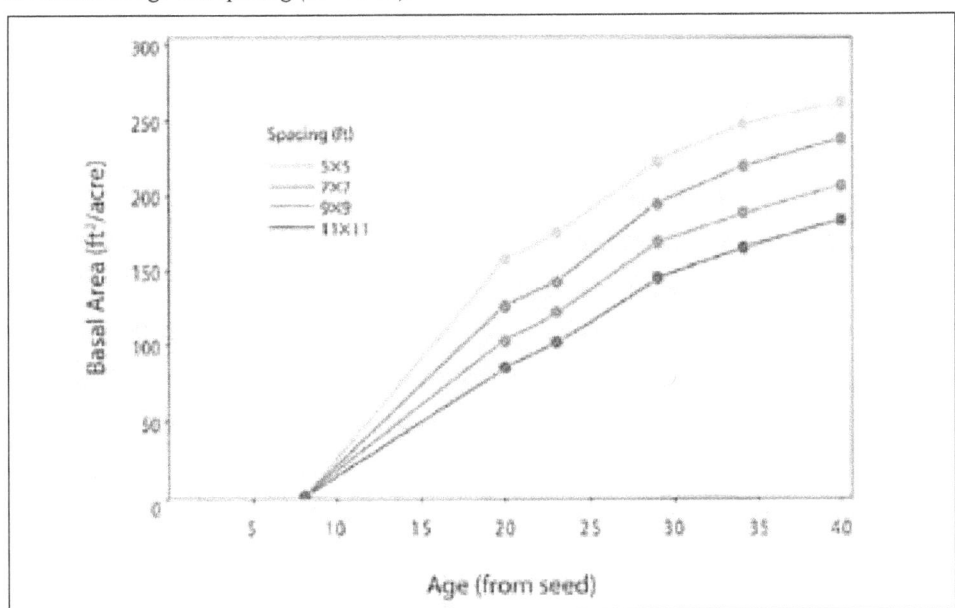

We should note, however, that BA accumulations approaching age 40, especially at the closest spacings, are at high-risk for suppression mortality, suggesting that relationships among spacings could soon change. Close spacing at young ages could have important advantages if high biomass production is a goal of management, but this requires more silvicultural attention in order to capture those benefits while avoiding risks of excessive stocking (see example, Chapter 9).

With the benefit of hindsight, we could wish that this and other studies in young stands had been measured far more frequently up to age 20-25, perhaps at 1-2 year intervals, in order to better understand the dynamic nature of stand growth at these early ages. Characterizing young stand growth behavior in mathematical terms turned out to be one of the most difficult aspects of growth forecasting (Appendix III).

Growth Behavior—Older Stands

Next, we consider BA growth in older stands. Figure 11 shows the gross PAI (ft²/ acre/year) of individual observations for the Birch Lake Plantation Density/Thinning Methods Study for ages 55-60 (average 57). While this example contains less background variability than other sets of observations in this analysis, it displays a stand density/ growth relationship that fits reasonably well the entire dataset for older stands—that PAI at ages greater than 20~25 climbs rapidly up to BA 90-100 ft²/acre and then plateaus for an extended range thereafter. It is also a pattern of BA growth that finds substantial support in independent red pine studies (for example, Stiell 1984, Rudolph et al. 1984).

Figure 11. *Gross PAI (ft²/acre/year) for the individual density plots in the Birch Lake Plantation thinning study at age 57 (SI ~60). Notice the approximately equal BA growth rates at stand densities greater than 90 ft²/acre.*

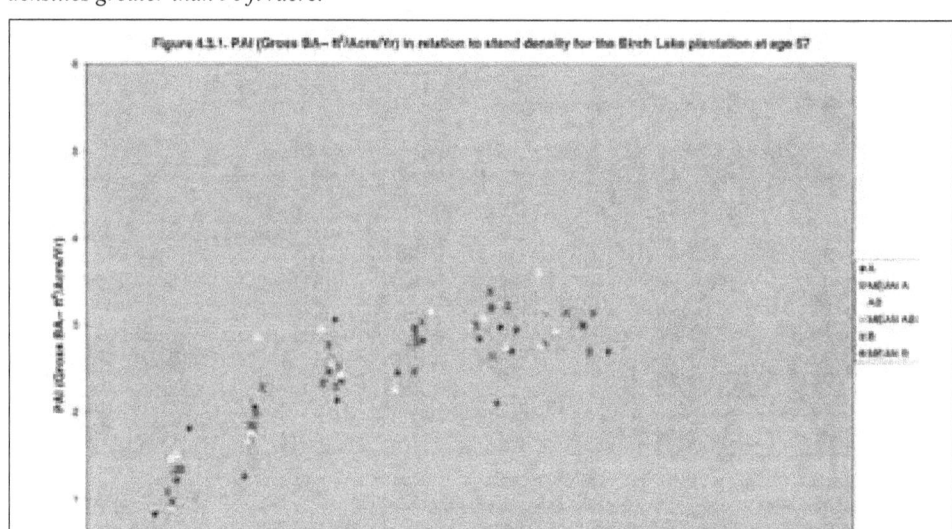

How does our growth model predict the effects of density on BA PAI through time for these older stands? In figure 12 we plot all BA growth observations for stands 25 years and older by 25 year-age groups. Superimposed at mid-age for each of the groups are the stand density curves derived from RP2005. Notice the plateauing of the curves in the density ranges of 90-200+ft²/acre. Notice also the wider dispersion of observations in the 25- to 50-year-age group. This is to be expected because there is much more growth variability at these younger ages and because the response surface is descending much more rapidly.

Stand Density and Height Growth

Let us now touch on two additional issues involving red pine stand behavior in relation to stand density. The first concerns height growth. Past studies suggested little or no difference in dominant height or height growth within the range of densities commonly used in red pine silviculture. This conclusion is generally accepted in field practice, although it is recognized that there can be local variations in the patterns of height growth (See discussion on site quality). An informal examination of data available in this study reinforces the conclusion that dominant height growth is little affected by stand density; thus, we have not pursued this question further, except to examine the consequences of thinning methods on stand height (Chapter 7).

Figure 12. *Gross BA PAI (ft²/acre/year) in relation to BA density for individual growth observations in stands 25 years and older, with median growth rates plotted for 5 age groups (assumed SI 55).*

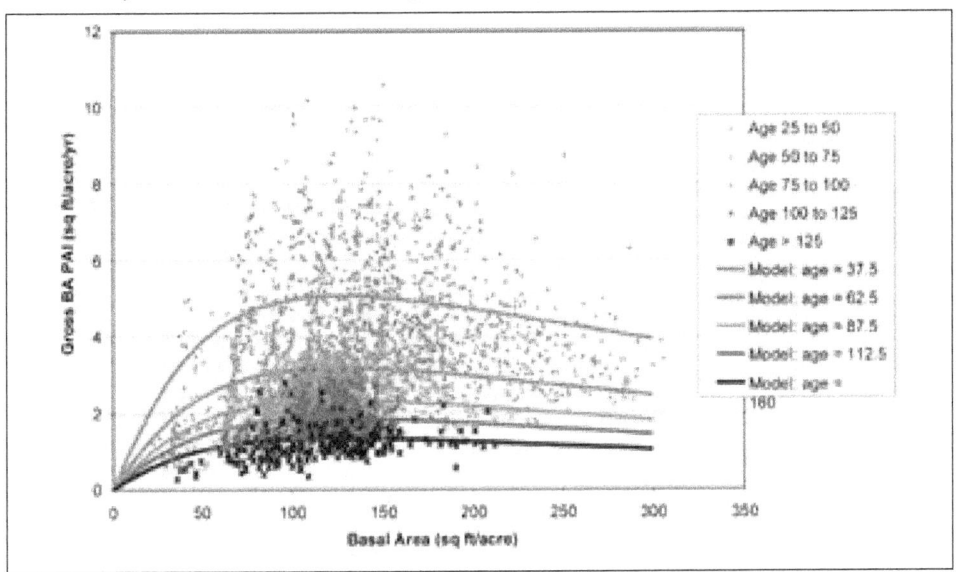

Stand Density and Volume Growth

The second question concerns volume growth in relation to stand density. Remember from previous discussion that: (1) dominant stand height is unaffected by densities commonly used in red pine silviculture, (2) BA growth is strongly influenced by numbers of trees up to about ages 20-30, and (3) beyond these ages, BA growth is relatively uniform over a wide range of stand densities. How does this play out in terms of cubic-foot volume growth?

The answer is that cubic-foot volume growth increases with higher stand densities, the magnitude of which is strongly influenced by stand height growth and to a lesser extent by rapid BA growth. This is because high density stands have more stems (or correctly, more basal area) upon which to accumulate volume associated with the height component of stand growth. These effects are most pronounced at young ages and high SIs, when stands are growing rapidly in both height and BA. The simple mathematics and geometry of this relationship were reported, among others, by Buckman (1962b). We illustrate by way of example (Chapter 9) some of the silvicultural and financial consequences of short-rotation, high-density management.

This finding—that cubic volume growth increases with increasing density—has been reaffirmed many times, not only for red pine, but for other even-aged species as well. It is only when stands reach densities suggesting the onset of suppression mortality that net volume growth may drop off. Even here, over extended periods, unthinned treatments in stand density experiments often accumulate higher cubic-foot volumes than the combined standing and harvested volumes of lower densities treatments. The challenge has been to quantify those relationships, and this too has and is being done for the important even-aged species worldwide. For this analysis, RP2005 is capable of estimating year-by-year PAI in BA (and cubic-feet and board-feet) for any reasonable combination of age, SI, and BA density.

A concluding note on stand density: BA is clearly a useful measure of stand density in older stands. Does TPA as an additional variable at these older ages affect the reliability of stand growth prediction? We examined this question for the 3,444 growth observations in stands 25 years and older. After the effects of age, SI, and stand density (in BA) have been removed, TPA in these stands adds almost nothing ($R^2 = 0.0033$) to the prediction of stand growth.

To recapitulate, at early ages, TPA as a measure of density has high predictive value for stand growth (for our study in the range of 200-3,000 trees per acre). Beyond say 25 years, it has little influence. However, TPA remains an essential variable throughout the life of the stand for characterizing mortality and for estimating the diameters of individual standing and harvested trees. RP2005 estimates QMD for a variety of thinning regimes, ages, and SIs.

Stand Growth Forecasting

With the background developed in the previous three sections, let us now merge age, SI, and BA/TPA density relationships into a comprehensive BA growth forecasting model. Here in the main text we use graphics and brief descriptive material to capture relationships, elaborating on the computer-based and mathematical methodology in Appendix III. As to approach, first we develop a model to predict gross BA PAI (ft²/acre/year) at all ages using BA as a measure of stand density; second, we model PAI in young stands using TPA instead of BA as the measure of density; and third, we merge the TPA and BA models, thus permitting stand density to be described in TPA at early ages and BA at older ages.

BA Growth Model

Figure 13 displays a 3-dimensional view of gross PAI (BA growth—ft²/acre/year) in relation to age and stand density on SI 65 land. A model with nine terms (Appendix III, p. 3-4) was introduced to satisfy *a priori* understandings of red pine growth behavior at various combinations of age, stand density, and SI. The parameters of this model were fitted by non-linear least squares, constrained to correct for anomalous behavior of SI curves (Appendix III, p. 7-8). The final model was statistically significant, accounting for about 85 percent of the variation among the 3,671 observations.

Figure 13. *BA growth model showing gross PAI (ft²/acre/yr) in relation to age (0-200) and stand density (0-250 ft²/acre) for SI 65 stands.*

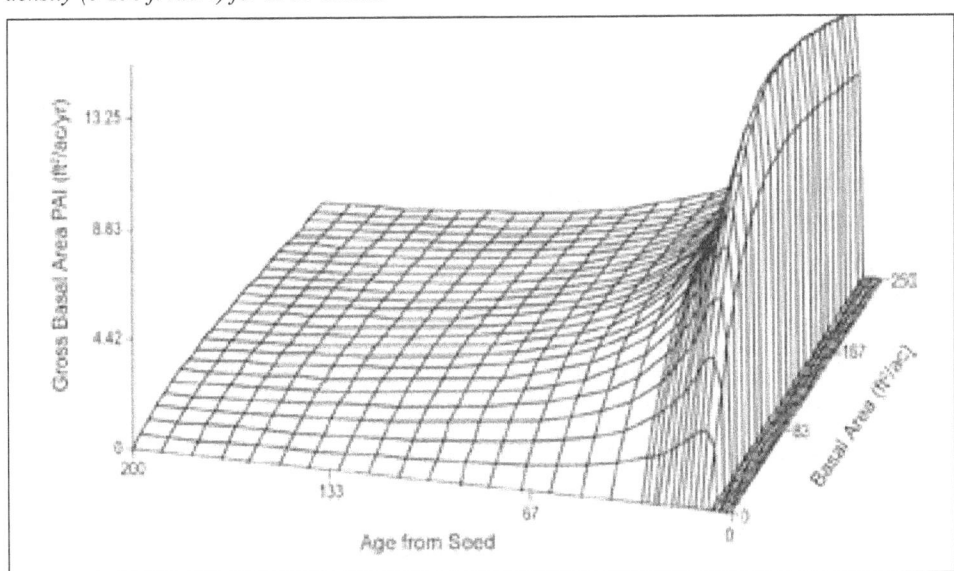

This BA model permits us to visualize for red pine the behavior of BA PAI (ft²/acre/year) over many combinations of age, SI, and stand density. Notice, for example, the attainment of breast height diameter at about age 8 for SI 65, and the rapid rise thereafter to culmination of PAI. Notice also the relative plateauing of the surface after approximately age 25 in the 90-200 ft² density range. Different SIs, of course, would raise or lower the surface.

The surface thus generated represents conceptually a key part of our understanding of red pine growth behavior and is the core component of the forecasting model. Keep in mind that portions of this and the TPA model display surface areas that are biologically impossible (notably at combinations of young ages and high stand densities). Also, remember that observations were limited, especially at the margins of both the BA and TPA models. Thus, there remain uncertainties about behavior of this surface, but it is consistent with what we know today.

The TPA Growth Model

Despite the fact that we can conceptualize and model reasonably well the life-long behavior of PAI in terms of BA, at young ages this measure presents both practical and theoretical difficulties. The practical one is that BA density is difficult to measure at these ages, when the stand has many small stems and low branches. The theoretical difficulty is that unrealistic or erroneous solutions may result when integrating these differential equations at very young ages when BA density is close to zero but growth is rapid. For these two reasons, TPA is more useful than BA as a measure of stand density up to about ages 20-30.

Figure 14. *TPA growth model showing PAI (ft²/acre/year) in relation to TPA for stand ages to 40 years on SI 65 land.*

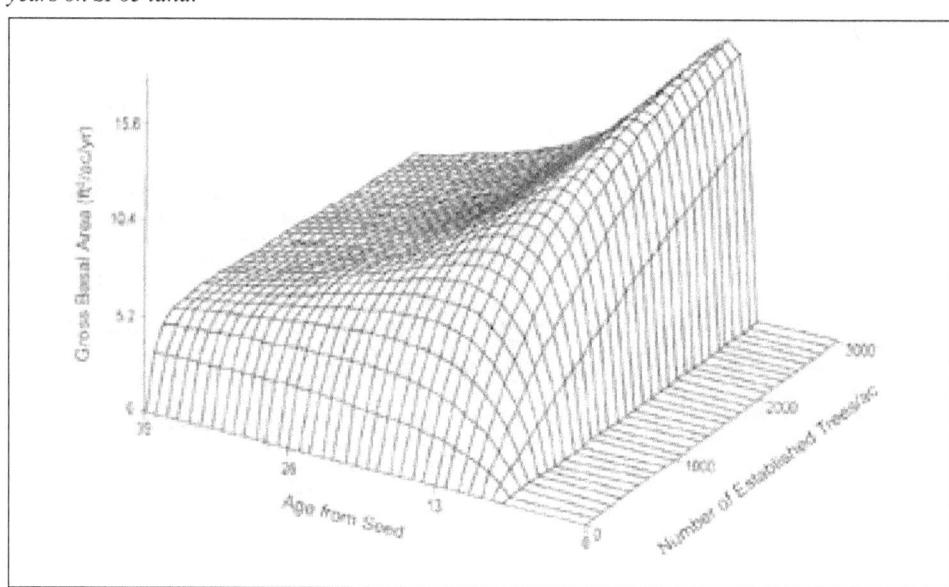

The TPA model (fig. 14) was estimated from 1,058 observations in stands up to age 50 (Appendix III). Because of fewer data and more variability, its R^2 (0.77) is not as high as the BA model but is still statistically significant. The challenge here is to use TPA as a measure of stand density in young stands and then to splice this function as smoothly as possible into the BA model as stands get older.

In so far as possible, we have adhered to the same concepts and assumptions in the TPA as in the BA model. However, under even the best of circumstances, it is virtually certain that regression surfaces of the two models will not join smoothly at the desired transition ages (20-30)—a juncture and age range that permits the most useful features of each model to be captured.

The Combined TPA/BA Model

We tested a number of rules to merge the TPA and BA models in the 20- to 30-year age range. The most satisfactory solution (described in Appendix III) effects a transition from the TPA to the BA model over a 20-year period. The resulting output is displayed in both tabular and graphic form in RP2005. Much of the PAI output, especially in the middle ranges of the several independent variables, will display a relatively smooth transition from the TPA to the BA model. In other cases, there will be a dimple or small discontinuity in the output graph where the two models merge. This disjunction will be of little practical consequence. Keep in mind also, in these transition years, there is little practical difference in using either TPA or BA as a measure of density; use whichever is more convenient. However, when both are used (required for tracking QMD changes) each needs to be carefully measured.

Summary

- Three factors, age, SI, and stand density (in BA or TPA/acre), have been and continue to be the most important variables for determining red pine stand growth through time. We examine each of them with a view toward better understanding their behavior. Following this we combine them into a comprehensive growth forecasting model for tracking stand BAs, volumes, and average tree diameters.

- Growth patterns at young ages (~0-25 years) present a different set of practical and conceptual problems than at older ages. This leads to a forecasting model (the TPA model) that uses trees-per-acre as a measure of stand density in young stands, and another (the BA model) that uses BA/acre as the stand density measure for older stands. The two models overlap in the 20-30 year range where either measure of stand density can be used.

- The combined TPA/BA model is at the heart of RP2005. Chapter 9 illustrates several examples of the kinds of questions that can be addressed with this model.

Chapter 4. Mortality

In the 1950s and 1960s we were unable to address in a meaningful way questions of tree and stand mortality since so little information was then available. Today we have a large data set, but are confronted with difficult methodological problems associated with the highly variable and unpredictable nature of mortality, and by sampling inadequacies. This is especially true in stands older than 80 years (fig. 15). Consequently, we develop what we hope are reasonable estimates of endemic (but not catastrophic) stand mortality and its effects on net growth. For the forest manager, however, there will still be great uncertainty in estimating the risk of mortality and of adopting mitigating procedures to lessen its impact. Managers can take some comfort in the fact that mortality in red pine is low compared to other Lake States tree species.

Figure 15. *Fallen trees represent endemic mortality in an unthinned portion of the then 85-year-old Bosom Field Plantation study near Roscommon, Michigan. Stand densities here are about 280 ft²/acre, near the upper limit of observed BA density for red pine. (Photo—R. Buckman).*

Of the 3,671 growth observations, 2,761, about 75 percent, have no mortality. Another 907 observations have mortality ranging from near 0 to about 5 ft²/acre/year, which we characterize as endemic (as contrasted to catastrophic) mortality. Only three observations, all in high-density unthinned plots, experienced partial stand collapse, losing nearly 40 percent of their BA in a short (average 5 years) growth interval. Two were in the Sooner Club study and one in the Birch Lake Plantation, all in the range of

250 ft²/acre of BA at the beginning of the growth interval in which the mortality occurred. Because the three "outliers" are so far outside the range of all other data and would seriously distort the estimates thus derived, we chose not to use them and instead to treat them as catastrophic mortality.

Ironically, an additional 246 observations in the database were in the 200-300 ft²/acre density ranges at the beginning of their growth period and, up to now at least, have not suffered such precipitous losses. They do, however, have substantially higher endemic losses than lower density stands.

A few notes about the magnitude and positioning of mortality in our database. The mean gross BA growth rate for all observation (outliers removed) is 3.42 ft²/acre/year. The mean BA mortality for the same observations is 0.114 ft²/acre/year, or about 3.8 percent of average gross BA growth. Partitioning the database by BA density, we observe the following: mortality averaged 2.9 percent of growth in the 3,425 observations with densities less than 200 ft²/acre, while mortality averaged 15.3 percent of growth for the 246 observations with densities of 200 ft²/acre or greater. Similarly, partitioning the database by age, we find that mortality averaged 3.6 percent of growth in the 3,500 observations in stands less than 150 years of age, while mortality averaged 18.4 percent of growth for the 170 observation in stands of age 150 years or greater. As one would expect, greater stand densities and advancing age increase the likelihood of endemic mortality as a proportion of total stand growth.

We need to keep in mind that there is also a large random quality about mortality that is not explained by stand density or age—losses from lightning, prolonged drought, or other weather-related losses, animal damage, or simply unknown causes—that can occur anytime in the life of a red pine stand. It is also highly likely that endemic mortality is episodic or uneven through time, for example, concentrated in years of prolonged drought or damaging insect populations, all adding to prediction uncertainties.

Estimating Mortality

Characterizing mortality mathematically proved difficult. We simply could not capture in one function a data set containing so many zeros, inadequate mortality information in older stands, and a highly skewed and variable distribution for the remaining observations. Instead, we adopted a 2-step process to address these problems (Appendix III, p. 98-101).

First, we estimated the probability of mortality at various combinations of age, BA density, SI, and TPA. All coefficients are significant ($P<0.0001$). Figure 16 shows the distribution of observations with (red) and without (blue) mortality in relation to age and stand BA. The two clouds of data show much overlap; the only obvious pattern is the greater occurrence of mortality at high BA densities.

Figure 16. *Distribution of stand growth in relation to age and BA density for the 2,671 observations without mortality (blue), and the 907 observations with mortality (red). Notice the broad overlap of the two swarms of data and the limited observations in older stands.*

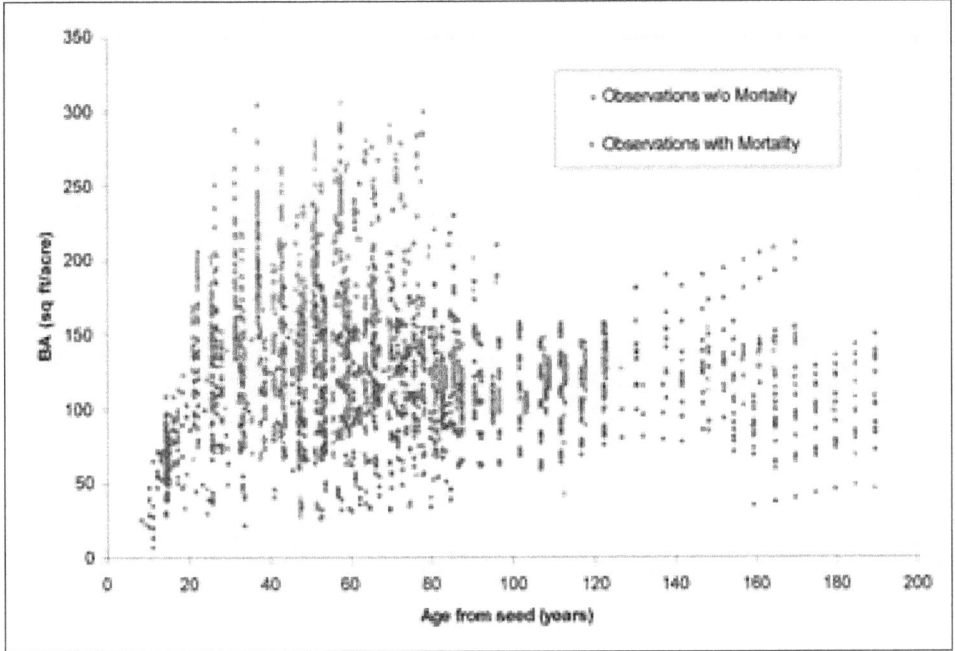

Second, for the 907 observations with mortality, we estimated a model of expected BA/acre/yr mortality in relation to age, BA density, SI, and TPA. This expected BA loss times the probability of its occurrence (step 1) provides an estimate of stand mortality at various combinations of age, SI, and stand density.

The resulting stand mortality surface for SI 65 is shown in figure 17. Despite the large error term (R^2=0.14), the surface generally behaves as one would expect—low mortality at low and mid-densities and at young and middle-ages, but increasing at high densities and older ages. The mortality function, subtracted from the combined TPA/BA growth function developed in the previous chapter, is the basis for estimating net growth. For any specified management regime table 2 of RP2005 provides estimates of mortality in TPA, BA, cubic feet, and board feet.

Mortality in a Larger Context

Discussions of mortality usually do not consider catastrophic losses—those that result from severe wind, ice and snowstorms, insect and disease epidemics, or from intense forest fires. Indeed, a portion of the Longview study (Appendix I) could not be used because of storm damage. Another stand density study in the Lower Peninsula of Michigan that otherwise would have been used in this analysis was entirely destroyed by forest fire before its first remeasurement. Additionally, the removal of three outliers from

Figure 17. *Stand mortality (ft²/acre/year) in relation to age and stand density for SI 65.*

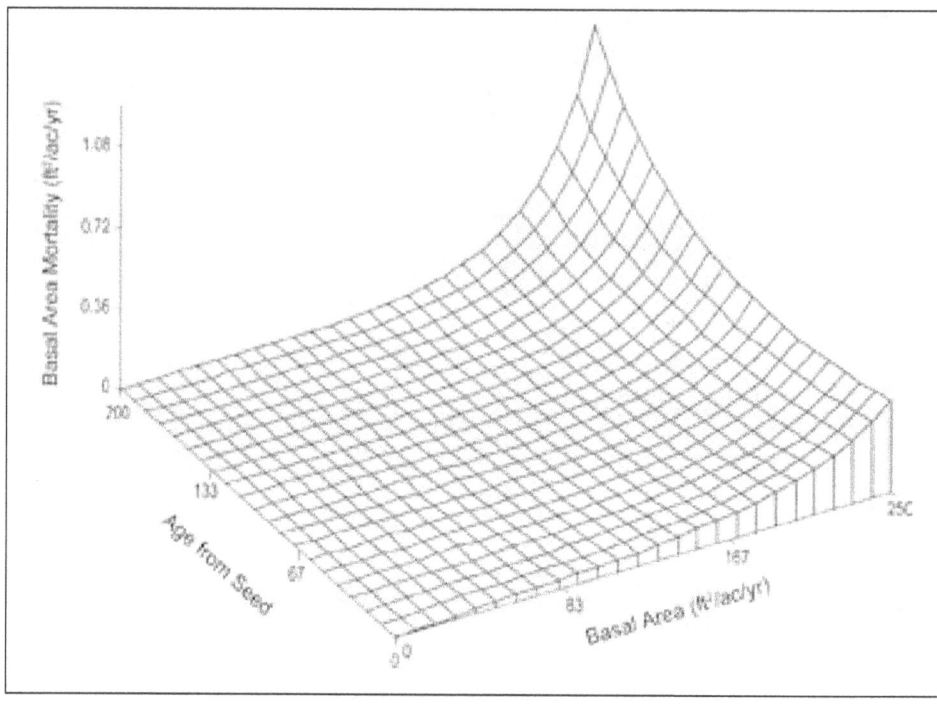

this data set is another case in point. Thus our database does not include catastrophic losses, hence underestimates mortality to some unknown extent.

Offsetting this is that land managers often develop a keen sense of impending mortality from such visual indicators as sparse crowns, insect or disease symptoms, injury from lightning, or from animal damage of various kinds. If catastrophic mortality has already occurred, trees often can be salvaged if stands are readily accessible (red pine is unusable for many purposes within a year or two following death).

Thus, red pine is characterized by low endemic mortality over much of the range of densities and ages used in most management regimes—in the neighborhood of 3.8 percent of gross BA growth per year for our entire dataset (and much lower at young ages and at low- and mid-range stand densities). As stands grow beyond a density of about 200 ft²/acre or 150 years of age, mortality increases, although, as yet, not very predictably.

We have not found a satisfactory method to estimate catastrophic mortality. We should note, however, from the most recent forest inventories of the Lake States, that estimates of red pine mortality (presumably including both endemic and catastrophic losses) is about 1.3 percent of total annual gross volume growth. This is the lowest of any species group in the region (Schmidt 2002) and lower than some of the estimates we develop for endemic mortality alone. All of this reinforces the notion that red pine mortality is low but highly variable.

We suggest densities immediately following thinning of no more than 200 ft²/acre, although users can go higher at their own peril. Furthermore, because our growth model otherwise permits stands to accumulate BA beyond any reasonable biological limit, RP2005 requires specification of an upper BA limit (up to 300 ft²/acre) beyond which a warning message alerts the user that this is the approximate upper limit found in both planted and natural red pine stands.

For the age dimension of modeling, we suggest an upper limit of no more than 250 years. The oldest stands in this study are about 190 years, but observations suggest that red pine stands may remain intact well beyond 200 years but with steadily increasing risks of losses from mortality. For some management purposes, extended rotations (perhaps in combination with thinning and salvage) are the desired goal. Even at ages approaching 200 years red pine stands on better sites are capable of producing 60 ft³ (~500 bd ft) or more per acre per year.

Two additional approaches to modeling mortality should be mentioned. The first is the exhaustive work of Buchman (1979, 1983) on individual tree mortality for several Lake States species, the most extensively studied of which was red pine. He developed probability estimates of individual tree mortality based on tree size and diameter growth rates. Not surprisingly, for the trees he examined (including some from the study plots used here), it was the smallest trees and those with the slowest radial growth that were most vulnerable to mortality. We use this work only indirectly because of the difficulty in translating individual tree losses into overall estimates of stand mortality. This study, too, found mortality losses in well-tended red pine stands to be very low.

The second approach involves self-thinning, sometimes referred to as the -3/2 power rule of self-thinning. It is a method that has attracted a great deal of attention over the past 20 years for several tree species, including red pine (i.e., Smith and Hann 1986, Smith and Woods 1997, Mack and Burk 2002). It has also attracted critics (Zeide 1987, 1991). The method involves estimating an upper or maximum size-density line (based on size and number of trees in fully stocked stands) beyond which stands are incapable of growing. The line has an approximate negative slope of 1.5 on a log/log scale, hence the -3/2 power rule. Parallel lines drawn at lower densities represent in ascending order zones of under-, optimum-, and overstocking. One then can track various combinations of tree numbers through these zones to obtain estimates of growth and yield (for examples see Smith and Woods 1997).

Our interest in self-thinning procedures was to search for stand density boundaries at which suppression-related mortality began and at which it became absolute—that is, beyond which net growth is zero. To test these possibilities, we prepared density management diagrams from unthinned plots in our datasets, following the procedures of Smith and Woods (1997). We then compared those results to the red pine examples given by Smith and Wood (their figs. 3a and b) and to relevant observations in our own database (i.e., fig. 16). For stands with larger and presumably older trees, we see a tendency (compared to our data) for the self-thinning approach to overestimate the BA densities at which self-thinning begins and at which it becomes total (or net growth is zero). For stands with smaller and younger trees, the tendency is the opposite. As critics of self-thinning rules have pointed out, the slope of the maximum density line is critical, and it is probably curvilinear rather than linear, thus accounting for at least a part of the uncertainty surrounding its use.

For forest plant associations lacking stand-management information, the self-thinning approach quickly provides operational silvicultural information to the user. However, we believe the prediction system presented here, based on growth estimates obtained from long-term permanent sample plots representing broad combination of ages, sites, and stand densities, and containing random as well as suppression-related mortality, better describes overall stand behavior. Our approach affords more opportunity, or at least makes it easier, to optimize the outcomes of silvicultural and economic options required to achieve any of an array of owner objectives.

A concluding note: The playing field for acceptable red pine silviculture is so large in terms of age, SI, stand density, and stand structure options that almost any thinning scheme will avoid suppression mortality. The flip side of this issue is that the approach presented here offers better opportunities to optimize outcomes.

Chapter 5. Tree Diameters, Volume Estimation, Financial Analysis

Let us turn to questions of merchantability—estimation of tree sizes and stand volumes. This in turn leads to economic considerations for which we introduce a section on financial analysis. In a later section we use this and related material to explore by way of example (Chapter 9) some important silvicultural and economic questions that can be addressed by the growth and yield model, RP2005.

Diameter Estimation

Stand diameter change through time is made up of two components: those due to growth (including mortality), and those due to thinning. To address the first, we derive mean tree diameter (QMD) from stand information produced by RP2005. In brief, this entails: (1) estimating BA/acre at a given age, (2) dividing this by TPA/acre at that age to obtain the tree of average BA, and (3) decrementing TPA by the numbers of trees that have died. From this procedure TPA and QMD can be projected through time. The TPA and diameter consequences of any of a variety of stand management regimes are displayed in tables 2 and 3 and figure 3 in RP2005.

The standard deviation of tree diameters is also carried in the detail tables of RP2005. This statistic is used to further define elements of mortality, sawtimber estimation, and diameter consequences of thinning methods

Diameter change due to thinning presents special complexities depending on how thinning alters stand structure. Here we encourage the reader to skip ahead to Chapter 7 on thinning methods and crown classes, where we examine the consequences of stand structure change on volume and diameter growth. See especially the discussion on **d/D** ratios, a quantitative definition used here to describe thinning methods. Can we capture these complexities with diameter simulation techniques? The short answer is yes—-RP2005 generates information to simulate these diameter characteristics (described in more detail in Appendix III, p. 91).

Table 1 of RP2005 requires careful specification of input information needed to estimate TPA and diameter change. At all stand ages the user must estimate TPA. At very young ages (up to age ~25) stand BA is generally too difficult to measure, in which case internal program calculations will estimate BA at these ages from TPA and other stand variables. At ages >~25 users should provide careful estimates of both TPA and BA. If the stand is to be thinned, the user must enter a **d/D** ratio for each thinning entry (ratio of QMD of trees removed to QMD of trees remaining). RP2005 tables 2 and 3 and figures 1 and 2 will display TPA and diameter changes through time for unthinned stands or for those thinned by any one of a variety of silvicultural prescriptions.

We need to recognize that diameter forecasting has shortcomings, including unrealistic outcomes for long projection periods, especially at and beyond the margins of data used in the construction of our model. **d/D** ratios are sensitive to faulty specification, especially for long rotations with several thinnings. One can argue that a tree model, for example STEMS (Belcher et al. 1982), as contrasted to the stand model used here, will be far more sensitive to diameter and diameter distributions. However, tree models are data demanding and are even more sensitive to forecasting errors than are stand approaches.

Two assumptions underlie diameter (and volume) projections. The first is that the QMD of the tree that dies is one standard deviation smaller than the stand average for living trees. The foundation for this is contained in Lundgren (1981) and further elaborated in informal studies (Lundgren 1999, personal communication). It reflects the fact that, in nearly all cases, the QMD of trees that die are smaller than the average for the living stand. The second assumption is that stand height is unchanged by mortality. This tenuous assumption is necessary because none of the studies used here recorded the heights of dead trees.

For all these limitations, RP2005 permits estimating mean tree diameter change in response to a variety of growth intervals and thinning regimes, and stand structure changes.

Volume Estimation

Total cubic feet is a more reliable predictor of stem and stand woody biomass than alternative measurement units, and the one we emphasize. From it can be derived conversion factors for a variety of products, not only cordwood and sawtimber, but veneer, chippable material, wood weight, and still others (for examples, see Snellgrove et al. 1984). We remain uncomfortable with the traditional stand-alone cordwood and sawtimber measures, reflected today in standards no longer as tightly observed as they once were. These changes can be attributed to higher product recovery resulting from improved technology and from increasing stumpage prices, both encouraging more complete utilization of all trees and the greater use of smaller trees.

Our earlier work (Buckman 1962a, Lundgren 1981) included estimating procedures for both cordwood and sawtimber. For this analysis, we provide an estimating procedure for sawtimber volumes, but have dropped cordwood. Today, for pulpwood products at least, there is little relation between cordwood estimates and recoverable pulpable material. Indeed, much of this kind of material now comes from smaller than specified trees, from tops of both cordwood and sawtimber trees, and from saw log residues. Additionally, short-term utilization practices are strongly influenced by fluctuations in market prices. We suspect that many users have already developed rules-of-thumb to address these and other merchantability problems for pulpwood. We should note, however, that cordwood measures are still used to describe 8-foot material used for reconstituted wood products or for small saw logs. Here the measurement problem has some parallels to the one for sawtimber.

Cubic-foot Volumes

For purposes of this analysis, cubic-foot volumes[3] are derived from a stand-volume equation developed by Buckman (1961): V=0.4085BH, where V=bark-free volume in ft³/acre, B=BA in ft²/acre, and H=average dominant stand height in feet. If B=<u>net</u> BA, then 0.4085=<u>net</u> volume; if B=<u>gross</u> BA then 0.4085=<u>gross</u> volume.

The total cubic-foot equation developed by Buckman continues to be used today. However, over the years, other stand-volume estimating procedures, both for total and merchantable cubic foot volumes, have been developed and could be substituted in RP2005 if they better meet user needs.

Converting total cubic-foot volume to merchantable volume, whether cordwood, sawtimber, weight, or some other unit of measure, is challenging. Over the years users have developed an imaginative array of rules-of-thumb and other ad hoc conversion techniques to satisfy their measurement needs. They will no doubt continue to do so.

Let us turn to predicting sawtimber volumes, the merchantability measure to which we give additional attention.

Sawtimber Volume

We adopt the red pine sawtimber utilization standards currently used by the Forest Inventory and Analysis group (FIA) of the North Central Research Station[4]. Essentially these involve three elements: (1) estimating the total cubic volume of each stem by one-inch diameter classes, (2) empirically determining the proportion of the total stem that is merchantable (for red pine sawtimber this is somewhat variable but approximates 95%), and (3) determining a board-foot/cubic-foot ratio by 1-inch diameter classes (ranging from 4.5 for 7- and 8-inch trees to 6.5 for larger ones).

Next we adopt a fairly complex set of procedures and assumptions described in Appendix III to convert stand cubic volume into sawtimber estimates. This in turn permits us to display in RP2005 board-foot output by age, SI, and thinning regime (International 1/4-inch log rule).

---

[3] Includes gross ft³/acre volume of all stems (bark-free), including stump, stem, and tip, but no branches. Based on table 3, Gevorkiantz and Olsen (1995).

[4] Unpublished information provided by Dr. Mark Hansen of NC FIA group, in turn based on a paper titled *Tree Volumes and Biomass Equations for the Lake States* (Hahn 1984).

Input table 1 of RP2005 requires the user to specify a minimum threshold size for sawtimber, say 7 (minimum), 8, 9 inches d.b.h. or higher. The board feet computation process is described in Appendix III (p. 101-108). Because so many assumptions and steps are involved, the user should be cautious about outcomes that suggest excessive precision and reliability.

Current practice for some users in the Lake States include measuring sawbolts (8-foot saw logs) in cords. If this is the practice, one may want to consider converting board-foot estimates to sawbolt volumes (measured in cords) by a conversion factor of his choice, perhaps 2 to 2.5 cords/MBF.

Financial Analysis

We address questions of economic analysis in the RP2005 tab labeled Finance. Here, for any of a variety of management regimes, the user can supply information tailored to anticipated costs and returns. The Users Manual within RP2005 elaborates on the details of data entry and output for financial analyses, and an example is given in Chapter 9. We follow the analytic procedures for financial analysis outlined in such references as Davis and Johnson (1987), Gregory (1987), and Pyhrr and Cooper (1982). We also call attention to economic work on red pine as outlined by Kilgore and Martin (2002), Harms et al. (1990), and Hyldahl and Grossman (1993).

Economic analyses demand a solid underpinning of growth and yield information and are equally demanding in their need for reliable cost and income information. Because so much uncertainty surrounds economic analysis, users may want to test run a variety of conditions to see how sensitive the outcomes are to these assumptions. While economic analyses are aimed primarily at private investments, public agencies can gain insights into questions of efficient use of capital, for example, by weighing the consequences of income forgone by extended rotations.

The analytic features contained in the financial section of RP2005 include Net Present Value, Benefit-Cost Ratio, and Return on Investment. A range of discount rates is permitted so that the user can observe the economic sensitivity of a particular management regime. Graphics are also provided.

Chapter 6. Wood Quality

Quality, defined here as the wood characteristics that determine suitability for specific product end uses, can be significantly influenced by silvicultural practices (fig. 18). Since wood quality was not a part of this analysis, we draw on the work of others to highlight some of the questions that one might consider. For those who want to dig deeper into the fundamentals of wood quality, we suggest such excellent references as Bowyer et al. (2003), Jozsa and Middleton (1994), and Gartner (2005).

Figure 18. *Cross sections at 4-foot intervals from stump to tip of a tree of average BA from 6x6 and 10x10 ft spacings 25 years following a precommercial thinning at age 22 in the "Graveyard Plots". Several wood properties can be modified by silvicultural practices, including knottiness, size of juvenile cores, specific gravity, radial growth rates, and tree form (See text below).*

Even without targeting product end uses, stand and tree quality can be markedly upgraded by traditional silvicultural practices. Perhaps the most obvious and effective practice is the aggressive removal of deformed, diseased, and otherwise defective stems, and, in mixed-composition stands, the species of lesser value, thus shifting growth to trees with higher product and value potential. Equally obvious, stand-density control and thinning methods can influence the size of trees harvested and those remaining for future harvests, thus working toward the desired size for many red pine products. Shearing of dead and live branches on standing trees by trees felled in thinning, especially in dense young stands, can be a significant and low-cost pruning agent, thereby enhancing lumber and veneer quality decades later as logs are processed.

For many landowners, these quality improvements, although not targeted at specific products and difficult to quantify, may be economically more important in the long-term than are volume gains associated with thinning.

To delve further into silvicultural influence on red pine wood quality it is necessary to think of specific wood products. As a general rule, wood for lumber is improved if the specific gravity is increased, if knots are eliminated or held to small size, if growth is slow enough to produce four or more rings per inch, or if grain angle is minimized. Working towards knot-free wood is especially beneficial.

For round timber products (poles, piles, posts, and cabin logs) bole straightness and modest taper are essential. Otherwise, wood characteristics useful for lumber are useful for round timbers as well.

For various panel products, desirable wood quality attributes depend on specific products. Wood especially suitable for lumber, for example, would also make good veneer and plywood. At the other end of the product spectrum, where wood is reduced to pulp or chips, quality is little affected by wood characteristics important for lumber. As we shall point out shortly, there is much evidence that a silvicultural strategy for reconstituted wood products would simply be to manage for high volume growth rates at low cost.

Other characteristics of products add complexity to this menu of desirable wood qualities. For example, the ability to hold paint is sometimes an important property of lumber or plywood. Red pine, like all abrupt-transition softwoods (Bowyer et al. 2003, call these distinct-ring softwoods), is not noted for holding paint well if the latewood bands are very pronounced; the problem is exacerbated in flat-grain panel products. Perhaps this wood property could be improved by silvicultural manipulation. For most round timber and some sawn timber, preservative treatability (usually under pressure) can be important. Sapwood treats more readily than heartwood, so for a given tree size, silvicultural manipulation that maximizes the sapwood/heartwood ratio might be desirable. Obviously, to tailor red pine to many of these products would require further study.

The number of wood-quality attributes that can be influenced by silvicultural practices quickly becomes overwhelming. For simplicity, we touch on only a few, including knottiness, specific gravity, radial growth rates, and stem form. How important the practice is depends on cost and the intended product. And, as a caution, if it is costly to modify management practices to improve wood properties, it is important for the owner to be able to capture the benefits at the time the wood is sold. Where return-on-investment is important to a owner, it is important to capture benefits early, sometimes difficult for red pine because of its slow starting characteristics.

Knottiness

The practical silvicultural techniques to reduce knottiness are either to reduce spacing among trees to diminish the size of live branches and the persistence of dead ones, or to prune branches as early as feasible in the life of the tree. Knot whorls, especially pronounced in red pine, are much more downgrading in lumber, veneer, and round timber than are scattered knots.

In his study of initial spacing in red pine plantations in the Lake States, Wambach (1967) found that initial stand densities of 400-2,000+ trees/acre had no significant effect on the average number of branches per whorl from breast height to 20 feet above the ground. However, Wambach found more branches per whorl on the better sites. As SI increased from 40 to 70, the number of branches per whorl increased from 4.3 to 5.9. A rough estimate indicates the number of whorls in a 16-foot butt log ranges from 16 on SI 40 to 9 on SI 70 (Lundgren 1981, table 3). Thus, even though the average number of branches per whorl increases on better sites, the number of branches per foot of stem decreases because there are fewer whorls due to greater height growth.

Wambach also found that the average diameter of dead branches (measured 1 inch from the stem) increased as initial stand density decreased, as site quality increased, and as distance from the ground increased. But the differences in average branch diameter were not large over a wide range of stand conditions. For example, an increase in initial density from 200 to 1,200 TPA reduced average branch diameter at the same height by only 0.25 inches.

Laidly and Barse (1979) found, at age 20 in the Spooner Plantation Spacing Study, that trees at all spacings from 5 to 11 feet (corresponding to 1,742 TPA and 360 TPA, respectively) had the same number of dead and live branches, confirming Wambachs' findings that spacing had little influence on number of branches on a given site (here SI 65-70). Live and dead branch diameters at a height range of 9-17 ft increased with spacing from 0.7 inches at the 5-ft spacing to 1.1 inches at the 11-ft spacing. Mean knot surface (the sum of branch diameters 1 inch from the bole) increased with spacing, from 3.8 inches at 5-ft spacing to 6.0 inches at the 11-ft spacing.

In some products, aggregate knot diameter in a short length (often 1 foot) is a measure of acceptable quality. Stiell (1966) reported that red pine with 220 TPA at ages 28 and 37 accrued, respectively, aggregate knot diameters of 9.6 and 10.7 inches in a one foot section. In this wide spacing, the sum of knot diameters exceeded that allowed for certain standard utility poles.

Pruning remains an alternative to reduce or eliminate knots, especially in the lower portions of the bole. Although not documented, observations suggest that the felling of trees in early-thinning tends to shear some of the live and, especially, dead branches on the remaining standing trees. Hand or mechanical pruning, practiced unevenly over the years by public and private owners, is another way to enhance product value in lower stems. Here, unless long-term records are kept and/or logs are graded at the time of sale and there is a substantial price differential, most of the benefits of branch removal are captured by those who own the logs at the time of processing, not by those who incurred the costs of pruning 30-40 years earlier.

The story of branch characteristics and their consequences for red pine products remains incomplete. The limited studies thus far have been confined to lower boles of trees in plantations. And yet, larger and more persistent live and dead branches are common in middle and upper boles in older plantations, and even more so in natural stands. This in part reflects crown size and behavior, themselves subject to some silvicultural control, although as yet little studied in middle- and older-aged stands.

Specific Gravity

Specific gravity is the quality characteristic most often studied in red pine as it is for other important commercial species. Attention invariably focuses on juvenile wood, the inner core formed by the first 15-20 rings outward from the pith over the entire length of the stem. Here growth rings are widest, latewood (or summerwood) proportion the smallest, fiber length the shortest, and fibril angle of individual cell walls the greatest—all associated with reduced specific gravity. Where strength and dimensional stability are the wood properties of choice, reducing juvenile wood content of individual stems may be an objective of management. For other wood uses, such as maximum fiber yield or pulp production, amount of juvenile wood may be less important than previously thought, supported today by pulping processes tailored to specific paper products (Bowyer et al. 2003).

A dozen or more studies have addressed specific gravity questions in red pine, summarized by Lundgren (1981) and Laroque and Marshall (1995). The individual investigations differ widely in approach and methodology but generally conclude that, while tighter tree spacing and advancing age from the pith (as contrasted to total tree age) somewhat reduces the size of juvenile cores and thus the average specific gravity of the tree, the consequences are much reduced once trees reach merchantable size.

Perhaps the most detailed study for red pine is by Laroque and Marshall (1995) at the Petawawa National Forest Institute in which they analyze individual growth rings between ages 10 and 38, with initial stand densities ranging from approximately 110 to 2,700 TPA. They conclude that spacing does indeed significantly affect relative density (similar in consequence to specific gravity) up to age 40 or so. This relationship is due less to juvenile wood than to the larger proportion of earlywood (which has lower relative density) than latewood in fast-growing trees. The closest spacing (2,700 TPA or 4x4 foot spacing) achieved a breast-high relative density of 0.40 at age 24, the 435 TPA attained this wood density at age 30, the 110 TPA had not quite reached this relative density by the end of the study at age 36. The trend in this study is similar to other research, but more pronounced. Whether it is important or not is unclear. One should note that the closest initial spacing (about 4 ft) and widest (about 20 ft) used in this study are outside the range of spacing normally used in red pine silviculture.

We should keep in mind that the specific gravity profiles of individual trees do not equate to stand yields in, say, total weight or fiber production per acre. Maeglin (1967), for example, reported little difference in specific gravity of individual stems in a red pine spacing study (11,000; 2,700; 1,200; and 680 TPA or 2x2, 4x4, 6x6, and 8x8 foot spacings, respectively). However, the highest gross yields at age 15 (when the study was examined) came from the 11,000 TPA, but the greatest usable volume (to a 3-inch top diameter) at this age shifted to the 1,200 TPA plots. Past research has shown great variation in spacing/specific gravity relations among the distinct-ring softwoods (Bowyer et al. 2003). Still, because specific gravity differences are not large, and juvenile cores occur in only the first 15-20 years outward from the pith, we can conclude that the per-acre weight and fiber yields for this group of softwoods will closely parallel cubic-foot volume yields.

Radial Growth

Radial growth rates outside the juvenile core do not appear to strongly limit end uses for red pine except as they influence tree size. Among the more than 3,600 growth observations in this study, diameter growth rates of the tree of QMD (at breast height) in excess of 0.50 inches/year (4 or fewer growth rings/inch) were few and were confined to juvenile wood of very young, low stand density, and high site stands. Many growth observations out to age 100 were in the range of 0.25 to 0.40 inches (5 to 8 rings/inch), which does not appear to detract from product quality.

Because tree size is important and so readily influenced by silvicultural practices, RP2005 permits tracing mean diameter growth through a number of stand management alternatives (with due caution about assumptions) including thinning methods.

Stem Form

Stem form is strongly influenced by crown position and clear bole length (Larson 1963). The greatest taper occurs from the base of the live crown to the apex. Crown size lends itself to silvicultural manipulation by density control and pruning, although this has been examined primarily in young stands (Stiell 1966, Stiell and Berry 1977). As Larson points out, stem form tends to be self-correcting through time, as the base of the crown retreats upward under stand-grown conditions and as height growth diminishes. Variable-form taper functions have been prepared for plantation-grown red pine by Newnham (1988), describing stem profiles, including butt swell, for those who wish to pursue this question further.

Quality—A Summary

For a tree with as much product versatility as red pine, knottiness, specific gravity, growth rate, stem form, and other attributes of wood quality play out in a variety of ways, depending on the uses to be made of the wood. One needs to look at specifications for a specific product to develop a sense of the importance of controlling any attribute, if it can indeed be significantly controlled by silvicultural practice.

For example, red pine has long been used for utility poles. Minimum strength requirements and specifications for each class of pole have been established by the American National Standards Institute (ANSI). For red pine the most difficult to meet specifications are circumference at ground line, top diameter inside bark, and straightness. Beyond these, sum of knot surfaces in inches in any 1-foot section and maximum size of a single knot face become limiting, although seldom so in managed stands. Minimum number of rings per inch may be specified, but is almost never limiting in red pine. Specific gravity of both mature and juvenile wood are indirectly reflected in pole size, which translates into slightly larger diameter requirements for red pine than, for example, southern pines, but smaller than for western red cedar.

Similar but more complex stories exist for such end uses as sawn lumber, glulam beams, plywood, structural flakeboard, and other products. The specifications and requirements for each of these uses have been spelled out, usually in industry standards backed by the American Society for Testing and Materials (ASTM), ANSI, standards of the Department of Defense, and other sources. The Forest Products Laboratory's Wood Handbook (USDA Forest Service 1999) is a good reference leading the reader to existing standards. Silvicultural strategies to enhance the performance or value of end uses need to be developed on a case-by-case basis.

A concluding observation: Many if not most managers of red pine will have at best an unclear vision about what products will be harvested from their forests, much less the strategies to maximize those outputs. Because of these uncertainties, the reality of red pine silviculture for most owners will be a middle-of-the-road strategy designed to keep open an array of options. This might play out with initial spacing densities of, say, 600 to 1,200 trees per acre (approximately 6- to 8-ft spacing) and BA thinning densities in the range of 100-140 ft²/acre. Those interested in greater biomass output and more stems per acre will operate at the upper end of those ranges; those who favor larger-diameter trees will work at the lower end. Flexibility in thinning methods, reviewed in the next section, offers great opportunities within these broad boundaries to respond to spot markets that favor products from larger or smaller trees.

Chapter 7. Thinning Methods and Crown Classes

Four long-term studies examined here were aimed specifically at thinning methods (above, below, above-and-below). In addition, crown classes were assigned to trees in these and most other post-WWII red pine studies. We explore these subjects in more depth than others in this analysis because so little has been reported on growth responses for either thinning methods or crown classes. The findings reported here suggest flexibility heretofore not fully employed in red pine silviculture.

In essence, we are asking the consequences of altering stand structure to favor retention of large, mid-sized, or small trees. Emerging is a consistent and reinforcing pattern of growth responses among both thinning methods and crown classes that suggests where growing space is ample, the smaller trees capture a disproportionately larger share of stand growth. Conversely, when growing space is crowded, the larger trees enjoy a growth advantage. Unfortunately, while the direction of the response is consistent, estimating its magnitude remains elusive.

As to approach, first, we examine growth responses to thinning methods based on four long-term studies. Next, to determine where growth occurs within the stand structure, we compare crown class responses, first, by thinning methods and second, by stand densities including unthinned treatments. We then compare these responses to those in the Portage Lake plots, an independent long-term density study in a natural stand. Last, we summarize the thinning methods/crown class analyses and explore the managerial implications resulting there from.

Thinning Methods

Four of the 31 studies (Appendix I) involve thinning methods, all thinned two or more times over a 32- to 45-year span. The Cutfoot study is in a natural stand originating in 1870. It has only one density (100-120 ft²/acre). The Birch Lake and Sooner Club studies are in plantations originating (from seed), respectively, in 1912/13 and 1929. These two studies permit comparisons of both thinning methods and stand densities. The fourth study, Bosom Field, is in a 1910 plantation. It was only thinned from above, but could be compared with adjacent density studies thinned from-below. The first three studies were replicated three times, thus permitting statistical analysis. Bosom Field is unreplicated.

Thinning methods are defined as follows: above, removal of dominants and codominants; below, removal of suppressed, intermediate, and smaller codominants; and a combination above-and-below, removal of approximately equal basal area in dominants on one hand and suppressed and intermediate trees on the other, favoring codominants. If we describe thinning methods as the ratio of the diameter (QMD) of trees harvested **d** to the diameter of the trees remaining after thinning **D**, then the **d/D** ratio for thinning from above is in the approximate range of >1.0 to 1.2; above-and-below, 0.9 to 1.1; and below, 0.8 to <1.0. Please note that we use these ratios and the number of trees associated with them to project tree diameters (QMD) through time (see **d/D** ratios later in this chapter and diameter estimation explored earlier in Chapter 5).

An examination of the plot records (and early participation by the senior author in two of the studies) suggests that conscientious efforts were made to maintain high contrast among treatments, modifying them only if a serious maladjustment of tree spacing might occur.

Basal Area Growth

Table 1 displays the cumulative net and gross BA growth to date over the active life of each of the long-term studies. All four studies permit us to compare thinning-method responses in the middle range of initial stand densities (90-120 ft²/acre), a density interval commonly used in red pine thinning practice.

Notice in these mid-range densities the consistent pattern of higher cumulative BA growth for thinning-from-above compared to thinning-from-below. For each of the three replicated studies these differences are significant (P<0.01). However, among studies, the magnitude of responses is variable for as yet unexplained reasons. Over 45 years, for example, the Cutfoot study has grown 38 percent more net BA on the above- than below-treatment. Bosom Field and Birch Lake are intermediate, with a 7-16 percent advantage over a 35-36 year span. And the Sooner Club study, at these mid-range densities, shows a 2-4 percent advantage over a 37-year period.

Thinning methods can be compared at lower stand densities for the Birch Lake (30- and 60-ft²/acre) and Sooner Club (60-ft²/acre) studies. Here the relative advantage of above versus below thinning is greater and more consistent than in mid-range densities. For the Birch Lake plantation, net BA growth over the 35-year period was, respectively, 25 and 22 percent higher for the 30- and 60-ft²/acre densities in the above- than for the below-treatment. For Sooner Club over 37 years the 60-ft²/acre thinned-from-above treatment had a 16 percent advantage over below.

Two things to note at these lower densities: First, these stands, unfortunately, were thinned only twice as compared to three times for the higher densities. This should make little differences in relative growth responses among thinning methods. However, the magnitude of the growth responses may be increased somewhat because it will take more time between thinnings for these low densities to recover. Second, in absolute as contrasted to relative terms, regardless of thinning method, these lower densities accumulate less BA and considerably less cubic volume growth than do their higher density counterparts (See discussion on stand density relationships in Chapter 3). Still,

Table 1. *Cumulative net and gross BA growth for four long-term thinning methods studies in red pine. The two right-hand columns contrast above- vs. below-thinning methods.*

Basal area After Thinning	Number of Thinnings	Basal Area Growth When Thinned From:						Above as a Percent over Below	
		Below		Above and Below		Above			
		Net	Gross	Net	Gross	Net	Gross	Net	Gross
ft²/acre	Number	ft²/acre						Percent	
Cutfoot -- 45 Year Summary									
100-120	4-5	80.8	82.0	89.7	93.1	111.9	115.5	38	41
Birch Lake -- 35 Year Summary									
30	2	52.0	52.4	65.7	65.7	64.9	71.8	25	37
60	2	87.3	88.6	100.6	104.3	106.2	111.6	22	26
90	3	95.7	95.7	101.8	104.5	110.8	112.3	16	17
120	3	101.0	101.0	93.0	112.9	108.1	110.1	7	9
150	3	113.8	114.8	102.3	111.0	110.4	114.1	-3	-1
unthinned	None	--Net 88.7		--Gross 111.5		----		--	-
Sooner Club -- 37 Year Summary									
30	2	89.7	91.0	--- No Treatment ---				--	--
60	2	147.5	147.5	145.5	147.0	170.9	171.9	16	17
90	3	172.3	172.3	166.5	167.1	175.1	181.3	2	5
120	3	169.3	169.9	148.5	166.4	175.8	181.2	4	7
150	3	165.0	177.3	--- No Treatment ---				--	--
unthinned	None	-- Net 57.3		--Gross 146.1					
Bosom Field -- 36 Year Summary									
90-120	4	144.2	144.6	-- None --		161.3	174.3	12	21

these results suggest that when ample growing space is available, the smaller (and more numerous) trees capture a larger proportion of stand growth than do larger trees.

Only the Birch Lake plantation contains a high density (150-ft²/acre) thinning method comparison. Here the differences among thinning methods largely disappear. In fact, gross (but not net) BA growth is little different from unthinned treatments. As conventional wisdom would suggest, at high densities and in unthinned stands, the larger trees survive and the smaller trees drop out.

As one would expect, the combination above-and-below generally lies between the above- and the below-methods.

It is suggested that mortality is greater in the above than in the other two methods. Indeed, it is likely that suppressed and intermediate trees in the above-method are more vulnerable to logging damage and environmental stress, tree classes that are otherwise removed where thinning is done from below. However, a closer look at mortality in the four studies suggests that low levels of random mortality and occasional pockets of high mortality associated with lightning strikes, bark beetle attacks, or unknown causes, occur across all thinning methods and densities, all apparently unrelated to thinning methods. Only in the unthinned treatments in the Birch Lake and Sooner Club studies (which may have 250 ft^2/acre or more of standing BA) are there elevated levels of mortality, most of which is associated with suppression. In any event, there is sufficient variability in mortality losses (excluding unthinned) that we are unable to detect statistical differences among treatments.

Cubic-foot Volume Growth

If we set aside for a moment questions of bias associated with height and stand structure differences among thinning methods, cubic-foot volume growth will respond similarly to BA growth, but somewhat more rapidly, especially at higher stand densities. Biases of a small but uncertain magnitude are introduced when we assume that average dominant height and stand structure are unaffected by thinning methods, and these heights and stand structures are subsequently used in volume equations. For the three thinning methods studies (Birch Lake, Sooner Club and Cutfoot), all thinned several times by the assigned method, the cumulative long-term impact (for the 60-, 90- and 120-ft^2 densities) has been to reduce dominant height 2 to 5 feet in thinned-from-above stands more than in the thinned-from-below treatment. This differential represents a nearly 6-8 percent cubic-foot volume disadvantage in these studies for the above as contrasted to the below treatment. Offsetting this bias somewhat is that SI determination is also based on dominant heights at the most recent measurements, thus reducing the apparent SI of the thinned-from-above treatment. This reduction in SI, in turn, is reflected in the growth prediction equations used in RP2005.

We are unable to address stand structure differences among thinning methods, but it, like height changes described above, deserves more study. However, in managed red pine stands, upper crown canopies are so uniform and the proportion of suppressed and intermediate crown classes (even in thinning-from-above) so small that this bias for most purposes can be ignored.

Tree Sizes

Thinning methods afford flexibility in shaping the size, quantity, and quality of trees, both harvested and standing, that, for some purposes, may be more important than differences in growth rates. To illustrate, table 2 shows some tree characteristics from the four studies—average tree diameters (QMD) before and after the first thinning, and average

Table 2. *Average tree diameters (QMD) at first thinning, and diameter and numbers of trees per acre at the most recent measurement for four long-term thinning methods studies.*

Basel Area After Thinning	Number of Thinnings	Mean DBH and Numbers of Trees When Thinned From:										
		Below				Above and Below				Above		
		1st Thinning		Most Recent Measurement		1st Thinning		Most Recent Measurement		1st Thinning		Most Recent Measurement
		Before	After			Before	After			Before	After	
ft²/acre	Number	DBH - inches		Number		DBH - inches		Number		DBH - inches		Number
Cutfoot --- 45 Year Change												
100-120	4-5	9.7	10.3	16.9	87	9.3	9.7	16.3	99	9.1	8.7	12.7	156
Birch Lake --- 35 Year Summary												
30	2	8.0	9.2	16.6	50	8.1	8.8	16.8	58	7.8	6.4	13.1	100
60	2	8.4	9.7	15.5	93	8.1	8.4	14.9	125	8.3	7.2	12.3	178
90	3	8.0	9.0	14.7	95	8.0	8.4	14.2	107	7.8	7.4	11.5	163
120	3	8.2	8.9	13.4	148	8.1	8.4	13.2	148	8.2	7.9	11.3	208
150	3	7.6	8.1	12.3	223	7.8	7.9	11.9	237	8.1	8.0	10.9	277
unthinned	none	Beginning DBH 8.3 inches--most recent DBH 11.1 inches, 398 trees/acre										
Sooner Club --- 37 Year Summary												
30	2	4.8	6.3	16.1	70	-- No Treatment --						
60	2	4.8	5.7	12.4	200	4.9	5.1	12.1	213	4.9	4.3	10.5	317
90	3	4.8	5.6	12.4	140	4.9	4.9	11.8	167	4.7	4.4	9.0	287
120	3	4.8	5.3	10.2	287	4.5	4.5	10.5	257	4.6	4.5	8.4	427
150	3	4.7	4.7	9.8	375	-- No Treatment --						
unthinned	none	Beginning DBH 5.3 inches--most recent DBH 8.4 inches, 573 trees/acre										
Bosom Field --- 36 Year Summary												
90-120	4	6.3	6.7	13.6	NA	-- No Treatment --				5.2	4.7	8.5	NA

[1] Small anomalies in tree numbers and tree sizes resulted from two thinnings at 30 and 60 ft. treatments as contrasted to three thinnings for 90 ft. and higher densities.

tree diameters and numbers of trees per acre at the most recent measurement. Notice that average tree diameters are significantly increased or decreased at the first thinning simply by choice of method, a condition that prevails (but is not shown) in all subsequent thinnings. Notice also the cumulative impact on the size and number of trees at the most recent measurement after three or more decades of thinning and stand density control.

Not shown in the table is the size of trees harvested, which could be larger or smaller than the remaining stand by 1 to 2 inches or more, depending on thinning method and variability of tree diameters. Stated differently, in older natural stands used in this analysis, two standard deviations (embracing 95 percent of the tree diameters, assuming a normal distribution) range from 5 to 7 inches. This suggests that the operator can alter the size of harvested trees by perhaps 4 to 6 inches or more depending on choice of thinning method and intensity of thinning. In younger plantations diameters are much more uniform, with 1 to 3 inches embracing two standard deviations, thus reducing the size range of potential harvested trees. Still, specifications for some red pine products are so tightly drawn (e.g., fence posts, barn and utility poles, round timber piles, house and cabin logs) that choice of thinning method affords useful flexibility even in young relatively uniform stands.

d/D Ratios

As we point out in Chapter 5 and earlier in this Chapter, ratios of the mean diameter of trees removed to the mean diameter of the remaining trees provides a quantitative dimension to thinning methods. We calculated the ratio of the mean diameter (QMD) of trees harvested **d** to the mean diameter of those remaining after thinning **D**. We did this not only for the thinning methods studies but for all other studies and growth periods for which there had been thinning, some 1,580 observations in all.

Growth residuals, that is the BA growth unaccounted for after the effects of age, site index, and stand density are removed, were determined for the 1,580 observations. A regression line fitted to these data slopes gently upward with higher **d/D** ratios, suggesting that thinning-from-above offers some small stand growth advantage over thinning-from-below. The R^2 for this relationship (0.017) is small. While the predictive value is low, the upward trend of the regression line is consistent with the findings of the thinning methods studies above—that higher **d/D** ratios (representing thinning-from-above) account for more BA growth than do lower ratios (thinning-from-below).

We then asked if the **d/D** ratio might contribute to the prediction equations for red pine growth. When added to the independent variables of age, site index, and stand density, it added 0.0025 to R^2, from 0.9352 to 0.9377. While this addition is statistically significant (because N is so large), it adds so little to growth prediction equations and is associated with such a high error term that we chose not to use it. Thus, while there is a consistent pattern of enhanced growth associated with thinning-from-above in managed stands, our ability to predict its magnitude at various combinations of age, site, and stand density is inadequate. For those who wish to explore alternative methods for quantifying thinning methods, Bailey and Ware (1983) offer a good starting point. They found that some of these ratios were significant predictors of southern pine growth.

Crown-class Responses

Crown classes were assigned to individual trees in many of the post-WWII experiments, following the classification methods developed by Gevorkiantz et al. (1943) (fig. 19). The system employs six crown positions (hereafter called crown classes), ranging from head dominants to suppressed trees, plus three crown densities. For our analysis, we used only the six crown classes, since crown class and crown density tend to be highly correlated. Unfortunately, this classification system was discontinued after the first two or three measurements, denying the opportunity to track long-term shifts among crown classes themselves. Little has been reported for red pine on this classification system except for a brief reference by Day and Rudolph (1972) and Smith (2003), which are consistent with the longer-term results reported below.

We track the BA of individual surviving trees from their most recent measurement back through time to their first measurement 30-40 years earlier. We then grouped trees by initially assigned crown classes, and for each of these cohorts computed the ratio of terminal to initial BA. These ratios (or percent growth) became the basis for comparing crown classes and treatments. In essence, we were asking, "What will crown classes observed today contribute to stand growth 5-10 years from now, 35-45 years from now?"

Figure 19. *Crown classification according to position and relation to surrounding trees. (After Gevorkiantz et al. 1943). Crown class O (open grown) absent on all studies.*

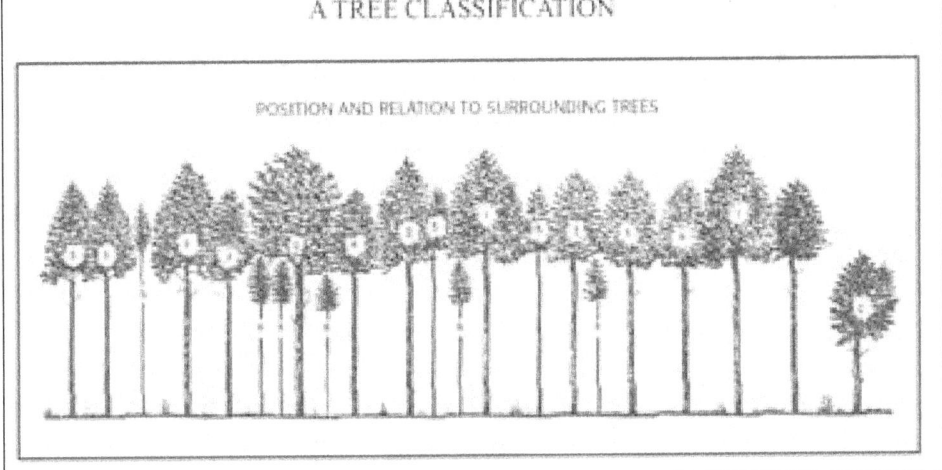

For short intervals, 5-10 years, nearly all trees survived. For longer intervals, 35-45 years, many trees were removed in periodic thinnings (or by mortality, especially in unthinned treatments). However, short-term responses by crown class were similar in direction to long-term responses, but lower in magnitude and somewhat more variable. For these reasons we emphasize here only the long-term responses.

Crown Classes and Thinning Methods

We first selected the Cutfoot study, the oldest of the thinning methods trials (45 years), for a more detailed examination of crown class responses. This stand, with essentially a single density, has been thinned 4-5 times back to 100-120 ft²/acre by the assigned thinning method. Plotted in figure 20 are the BA growth responses (in percent) for each crown class within the three thinning methods.

Notice the small differences among thinning methods, but the consistent upward growth trend toward smaller crown classes. Thinning methods here are not statistically significantly different from each other, but crown classes are (P<0.01).

We then similarly analyzed the Birch Lake and Sooner Club studies. Here we can compare crown class responses not only by thinning method but also by residual stand densities (30, 60, 90, 120, 150 ft²/acre). The results were comparable to the Cutfoot study. When crown classes were considered, thinning methods were not statistically significant at any of the densities but crown classes and density/crown class interactions were (P<0.01)

Figure 20. *Cutfoot Thinning Methods Study—45-year BA growth (in percent) by crown class and thinning method. (Note: 95% confidence band shown for each crown class.)*

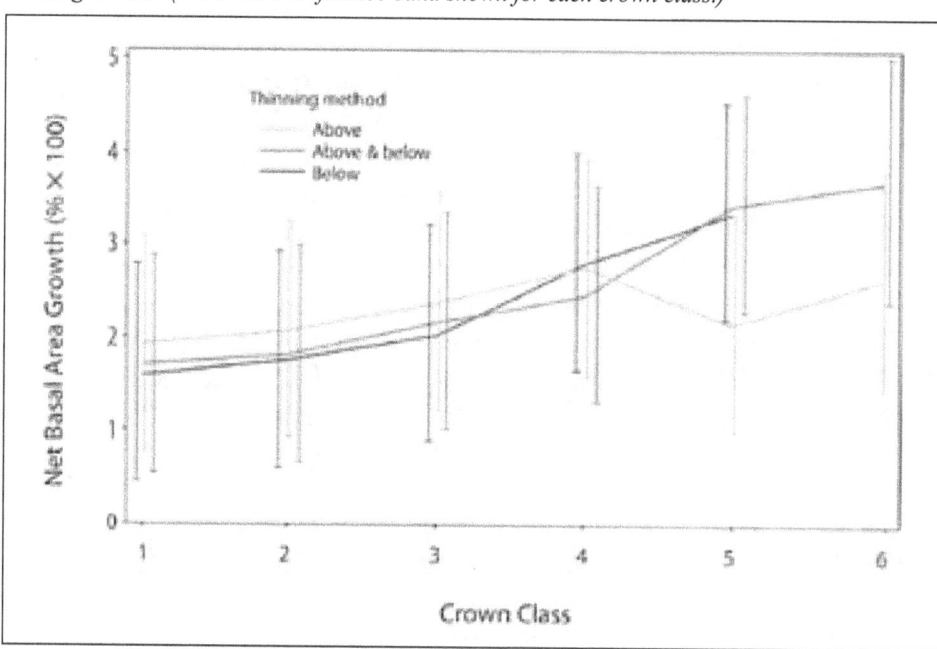

Because we were unable to detect differences among thinning methods when the influence of crown classes was considered, in subsequent analyses we combine thinning methods and focus only on stand density/crown class relationships. Let us dig deeper into this question.

Stand Density/Crown Class Interactions

Figures 21a and b display long-term BA growth rates (in percent) by stand density and crown class for the Birch Lake and Sooner Club studies. While these studies differ in some details, both contain three thinning methods (now combined), five stand densities plus unthinned controls, and have been thinned several times over more than 30 years.

Both studies indicated statistically significant differences for crown classes ($P<0.01$) and crown class/density interactions ($P<0.01$). Thinning methods, as we indicated above, did not significantly affect results.

We then chose the Portage Lake density study, in a natural stand with presumably more crown class variability than the plantations described above, as an independent test of these relationships. At age 54, the Portage Lake Study (BA densities of 60-, 80-, 100-, 120- and 140-ft^2/acre) was installed. It has been thinned, generally from below, two or three times back to the assigned BA densities over the 35 years the study has been active. The growth responses by crown class and density are shown in figure 22.

The pattern and direction of crown class/density response is remarkably consistent with those of the Birch Lake, Sooner Club, and Cutfoot studies. Differences in crown class and crown class/density interaction are statistically significant ($P<0.05$). However, while there are substantial similarities among all studies, the magnitude of responses differs somewhat and for as yet unexplained reasons.

An independent and compelling set of corroborating studies comes from Brand and Magnussen (1988) and Magnussen and Brand (1989) of the Petewawa National Forestry Institute. Employing techniques from plant competition research, they examined the growth behavior in three red pine density studies and achieved results similar to those reported here—that the distribution of stand growth among tree sizes is strongly influenced by density, with smaller trees losing vigor as density increases. Their research suggests an alternative analytic approach to the one used here; they too were able to quantify the direction but not the magnitude of crown-class responses associated with stand density.

Figure 21. *Long-term BA growth (in percent) by stand density and crown class for: (a) the Birch Lake, and (b) Sooner Club thinning methods studies. (Note: 95% confidence band shown for each crown class.)*

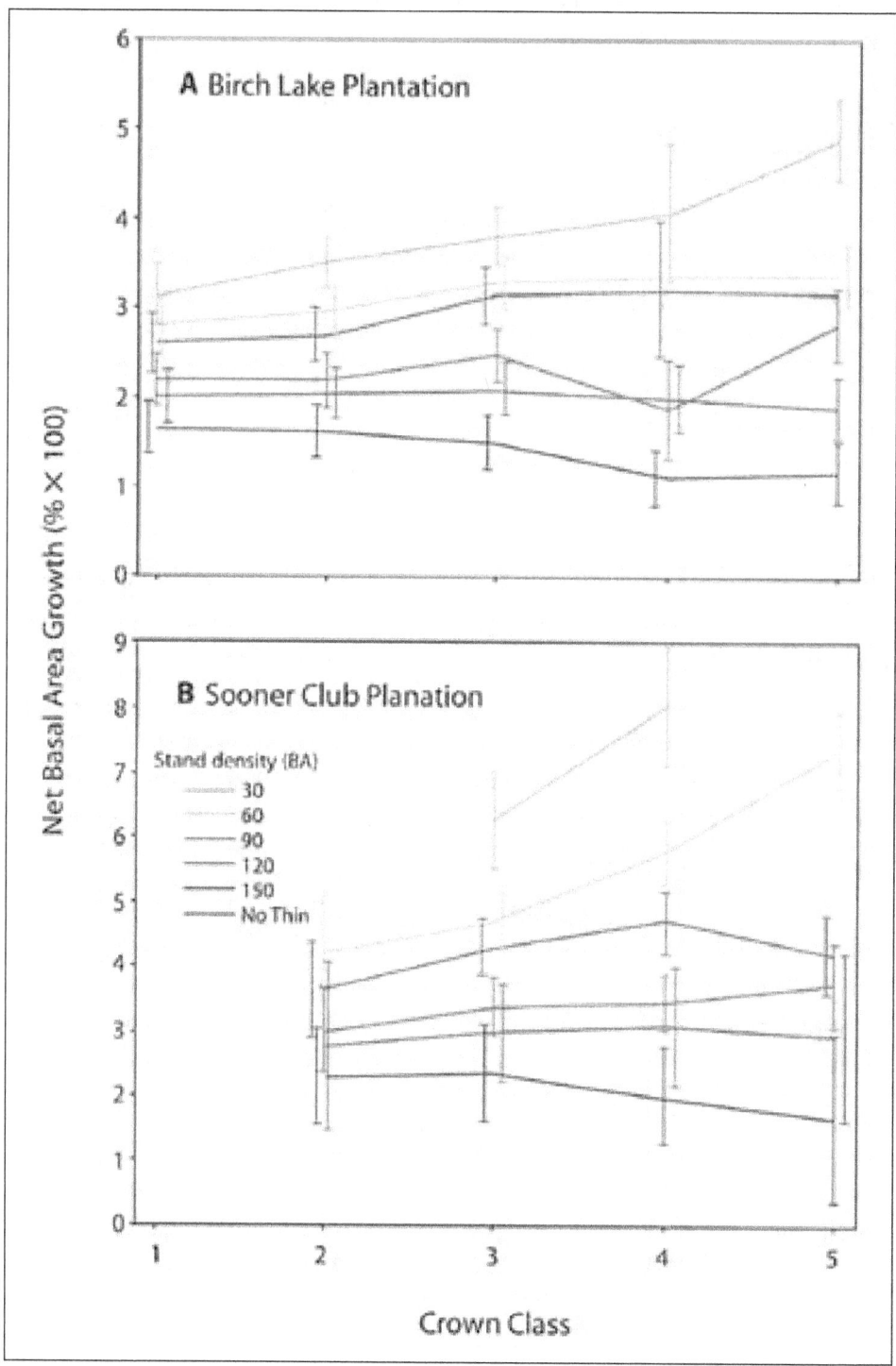

Figure 22. Long-term BA growth (in percent) by stand density and crown class for the Portage Lake thinning study. (Note: 95% confidence band shown for each crown class.)

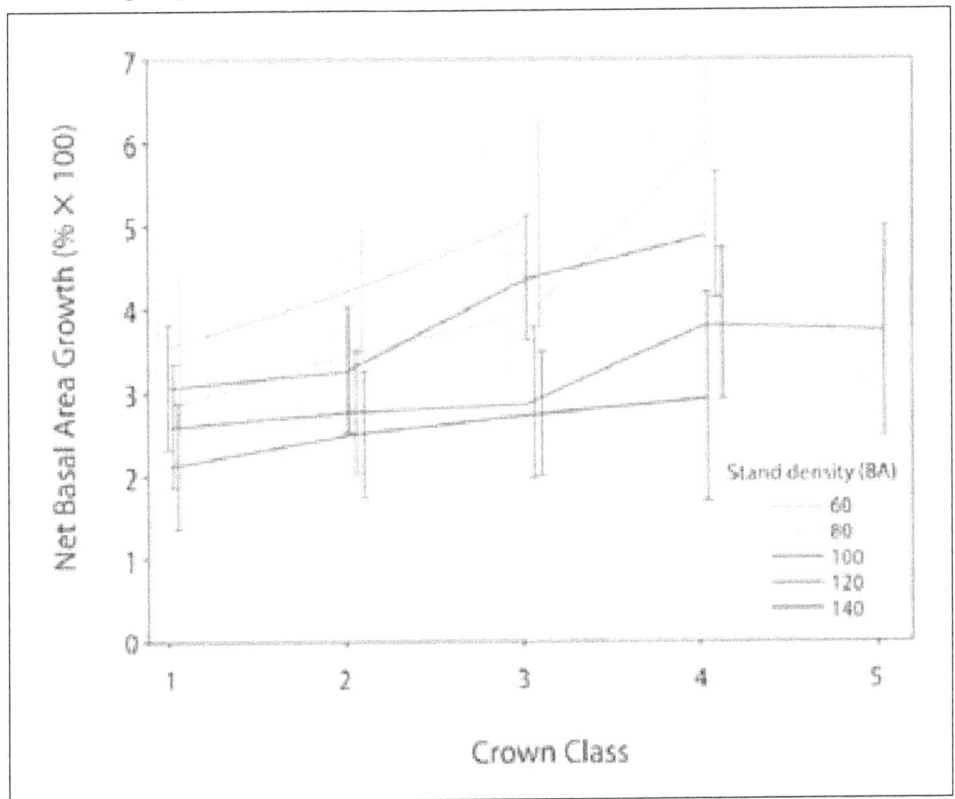

Summary

Highlights

Let us summarize the outcomes of these several studies with a view toward exploring silvicultural/economic consequences flowing there from:

- Thinning-from-above at low- and mid-levels of stand density consistently produced more net and gross BA growth than thinning from below. At higher residual thinning densities (120-150 ft²/acre and higher), differences diminish and finally become indistinguishable among thinning methods (table 1). The combination above-and-below method generally produced intermediate results.

- The magnitude of these BA growth differences at mid- and low-densities is always positive but variable. At lower densities (30-60 ft²/acre) the net and gross BA growth advantage of above versus below ranged from 16 to 37 percent (table 1). At mid-level densities, the advantage ranged from 2 to 5 percent in the Sooner Club study to as much as 38 to 41 percent in the Cutfoot study. The reason for this variability is not apparent, inviting more study.

- Cubic-foot volume growth (and merchantable volume growth modified by stand structure and product specification) follow the trends of BA growth, but is larger at high stand densities for reasons given in the discussion of stand density in Chapter 3. Small but difficult to evaluate biases are introduced from changes in dominant height and stand structure among the various thinning methods.

- Crown classes better explain growth responses than do thinning methods. Indeed, with more growing space (as in the 30- and 60-ft^2/acre densities), it is the codominant, intermediate, and even better suppressed trees that capture a larger proportion of stand growth (figs. 20, 21, and 22). Since more of these trees remain after thinning-from-above, both the crown class and thinning method responses are highly consistent. In practical silvicultural terms, however, implementation is probably more easily executed in terms of thinning methods (with some stand density constraint) than by crown classes.

- As stand densities increase (say, beyond 120-150 ft^2/acre), growth shifts toward larger crown classes. In unthinned stands it is the dominant and codominant trees that capture growth even as the smaller trees slow in growth and die (table 1).

- Average tree size, both harvested and standing, is substantially affected both immediately and in the long-term, by choice of thinning method and stand density (table 2). RP2005 allows the user to examine these diameter effects.

Silvicultural and Economic Implications

In historical terms, thinning-from-above was often equated with "high-grading." In those early years, emphasis was on harvesting products that would pay their way, which meant removing the larger and more valuable trees. There was little concern for the stand that remained. Over the years has come better care of red pine stands through improved planting practices, better control of competing vegetation, and more uniform spacing of trees. This in turn leaves the entire growing-stock in better condition to respond to an array of thinning methods. The several studies described here are located in such well-tended stands.

Other conventional wisdom embodied in this issue suggests that large trees—including big crowns—are best able to capture stand growth. However, our evidence suggests the contrary, that when ample growing space is available, it is the smaller and intermediate-sized trees (and crowns) that capture a disproportionately larger share of stand growth. An explanation for this is not readily apparent, but we believe that below-ground processes (next Chapter) suggest at least a partial explanation as to why smaller but more numerous trees are better able to appropriate site resources.

In any event, the four long-term studies described here suggest a larger array of silvicultural options are available to satisfy a variety of economic or other goals than heretofore thought prudent. For a tree as versatile as red pine, with ever changing product and price relationships, this becomes an additional and valuable source of managerial discretion. It is a complicated one, for the removal of one size class or another inevitably has consequences for the next and subsequent thinnings and for the final harvest. Still, the ability to remove (or retain) trees of one size class or another to satisfy spot markets may be among the most useful forms of managerial discretion available to the land owner.

Regrettably, we are only partially able to generalize about growth responses associated with thinning methods. The BA and volume growth functions contained in the text and in Appendix III reflect averages of thinning methods, not values for individual treatments. We attempt, however, to estimate changes in mean d.b.h. and tree numbers associated with stand structure changes using **d/D** ratios.

Chapter 8. Row Thinning, Thinning Intensity, Spatial Arrangements, Root Systems

In this section we explore several silvicultural questions that offer additional flexibility and discretion in managing red pine stands, although they do not play a central role in growth and yield forecasting.

Row Thinning

The 1950s and 1960s heralded the onset of commercial thinning from pre-WWII red pine plantations. It was also a period of rapidly evolving mechanization, generally leading to larger and more efficient harvesting equipment. This, in turn, suggested row thinning as a low-cost alternative to individual tree selection for the first entry in plantations.

In anticipation of these changes, three plantation thinning experiments included in this dataset were installed—Bosom Field in 1951, Sooner Club in 1960, and Ravenna in 1960—all in the Lower Peninsula of Michigan (Appendix I). They contained row- thinned treatments (every other row, every third row) for comparison with uniformly-spaced trees at several residual densities (fig. 23). Michigan State University (MSU) initiated two similar row-thinned studies, one on the Kellogg Research Forest in the Lower Peninsula in 1960, and the other on the Dunbar Experimental Forest in the Upper Peninsula in 1962.

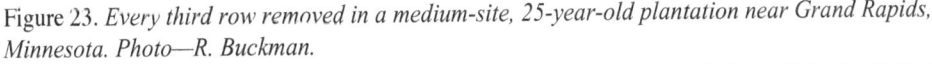

Figure 23. *Every third row removed in a medium-site, 25-year-old plantation near Grand Rapids, Minnesota. Photo—R. Buckman.*

The MSU studies contained several uniformly thinned density levels plus row thinned plots. The row-thinned treatments included every-other and every-third-row thinning, and two treatments removing every fourth row, followed 5 years later by removal of (1) the intervening third row and (2) uniform thinning of the three rows. The row-thinned plots have been thinned several times since the initial treatments, using individual tree selection to achieve uniform distribution of growing stock.

Emerging from these studies is a remarkably consistent pattern—long-term net and gross growth accumulations in row-thinned treatments are indistinguishable from uniformly spaced trees when both treatments maintain similar residual stand densities. Cooley (1969) first reported these findings for the Bosom Field, Sooner Club, and Ravenna studies. Our analyses confirm these early results. Nearly identical findings are reported for the two MSU studies (Day and Rudolph 1972, Rudolph et al. 1984).

Row thinning today remains the only realistic and economic means for first entry into most red pine plantations, and would be used by many managers even if there were modest growth penalties. Although not a part of this analysis, we can reasonably conclude that similar responses would occur in dense, young, natural stands that are thinned in strips. Removal of defective and poorly formed trees in the remaining rows or strips can be deferred until the second and subsequent tree-selection thinnings, with little or no long-term adverse consequences.

We do not distinguish between row and selection-thinned growth estimates in our growth and mortality equations.

Thinning Intensity

In earlier work, Buckman (1962a) asked whether intensity of thinning could account for growth (or lack of it) after the effects of age, site, and stand density had been removed. At that time we could detect no adverse effect. We ask the same question again, this time with more observations, some representing much more heavily thinned stands than in the previous study.

Thinning intensity is defined here in two ways: as square feet of BA/acre removed, or as the ratio or percent of the pre- to post-thinning BA/acre. Available for the current analysis are 10 times as many observations as available previously, 1,580 growth observations in all, which began with some degree of thinning. Most thinnings were light to moderate. Some were drastic by any measure, especially in several density studies, where BA/acre could be reduced from 150 to 200 ft^2/acre to 30 and 60 ft^2/acre in a single thinning. We test two measures of intensity: (1) BA removed, which ranged from near zero to more than 150 ft^2/acre, and (2) percent of pre-thinned to post-thinned BA, which ranged from negligible up to 400 percent or more.

Despite the wide range of thinning intensities, there was little or no predictive value in either measure, after the effects of age, site, and stand density had been removed. BA removed accounted for 0.6 percent of the residual R^2. BA removed as percent of the pre-thinned stand accounted for even less, 0.4 percent of the residual R^2.

These findings suggest, for stands of the kind represented in these studies, that there is little evidence of an adverse or "shock effect" from heavy thinning. This means that stands with reasonably sturdy and well-distributed growing stock can be thinned from a high to a low density in a single entry—that stands with a high proportion of crooked, defective, and otherwise poor-quality growing stock, or less-desirable species, can be greatly improved in a single thinning—all without undue concern for losing growth because of the heavy thinning itself. This finding points to more flexibility and aggressiveness in red pine thinning practices than we might previously have considered. Keep in mind, however, that lower stand densities rather than intensity of thinning will result in reduced volume growth.

It is always necessary to add the qualifier that some stands, because of high density, may be too tall for the diameters of the individual stems to support wind and snow loads following heavy thinning (too high height/diameter ratio). Such stands are found, but much less commonly than one would think. We should also keep in mind that red pine is perhaps the most wind- and snow-resistant conifer in the Lake States, and that these results must be used with caution for other species. And finally we should note that some degree of endemic or catastrophic loss is possible, even in the best-tended red pine stands.

Individual Tree Distribution

Since diameters at any given age are closely related to growing space available to individual trees, we ask whether the variability of tree diameters might indicate how well growing space was being used. We postulate that greater diameter variability reflects less uniform spacing among trees, hence less efficient use of growing space. Conversely, the smaller the diameter variability, as in young plantations, the better growing space is used.

To test this notion, we calculated the standard deviation (surrounding the plot arithmetic mean diameter) of tree diameters for individual growth plots at the beginning of each observation period. More than 3,500 observations were available. Standard deviations largely grouped in the 1- to 3-inch ranges, suggesting that about 95 percent of the trees (two standard deviations) would be contained in a 2- to 6-inch diameter range, assuming a normal distribution. Several of the older natural stands reflect still higher standard deviations, in the 4- to 5-inch range.

Standard deviation plotted against BA growth residuals (after the effects of age, site, and stand density had been removed) accounted for only 0.038 percent of the R^2. This suggests that diameter variability, or lack of it, contributes almost nothing to predicting growth behavior in red pine, whether in planted or natural stands.

Certainly, trees can be so mal-distributed that stand growth can be impaired. An example is contained in a thinning study started in 13 year-old red pine (Stiell 1982), in which growth was compared between trees in 4-tree clumps with those uniformly spaced, in both cases growing at 320 trees per acre. There were substantial differences in individual tree and crown characteristics between treatments 10 and 15 years later. After 15 years, BA growth was about 18 percent higher on the uniform compared to the clumped spacing, suggesting that this degree of non-uniform spacing can indeed produce differences in BA (and cubic volume) growth.

Root Systems and Below-ground Processes

Much silvicultural literature suggests that characteristics of tree crowns (size, volume, leaf area) are the principal driving mechanisms influencing tree and stand growth. Or, as Spurr (1952) wrote 50 years ago, "In crown studies, the assumption has been tacitly made in most cases that root competition is correlated with crown development. Although this is generally true, the degree of correlation is not necessarily very high".

Several findings from this analysis, combined with earlier research on root systems and more recent work on mycorrhizal (literally, fungus-roots) relationships, strongly suggest that below-ground processes rather than crown behavior better explain red pine growth. This is not to suggest that crowns are unimportant; rather that below-ground processes need to be considered much more seriously both in silvicultural practice and in future research.

First, let us consider several findings from this analysis that point to the importance of rooting zone activities more so than crown behavior:

- Inability of thinning intensity to account for stand growth after effects of age, site, and stand density have been removed (previous section, this Chapter).
- Importance of numbers of trees in accounting for growth up to about age 25 (during the time of rapidly expanding root occupancy), followed thereafter, presumably after full site occupancy, by the inability of tree numbers to account for growth after effects of age, site, and stand density have been removed (Chapter 3).
- Inability to distinguish growth differences between row-thinned and uniformly spaced-thinned stands of similar density (first section, this Chapter)

Studies of rooting zones in red pine have been few, no doubt because of the cost and difficulty of such studies. Day (1941) excavated the root systems of five 12- to 14-year-old red pines on two sites in the Upper Peninsula of Michigan. Vertical root development, including the tap root, was generally shallow, seldom exceeding three feet. Lateral root development on the other hand was extensive, reaching out from the stump one to three times the height of the tree. Stiell (1970) reported similar results from Canadian studies, describing one 27-foot tall tree in a 5x5 ft plantation spacing whose root system extended 47 feet in one direction and 34 feet at right angles to it. The roots of this tree invaded the space of 23 neighbors, and in turn were occupied by root systems of 11 nearby trees. It also had root grafts to two other trees. All of this points to overlapping and intermingled root systems that enable surviving trees to appropriate much of the available soil nutrition and moisture following removal of some of their neighbors

A second line of emerging research concerns the importance of mycorrhizal fungi (and perhaps root grafts as well) in sharing or otherwise capturing nutrients and energy among trees of the same and sometimes different species (Simard et al. 1997, Read 1997, Smith and Read 1997). Little research has been done in red pine on these below-ground processes, but it is an attractive area for further inquiry and for comparative studies among other even-aged conifers.

Information thus far available suggests that root systems of red pine, compared to other fast-growing conifers, are slow to fully occupy a site. Once they do, however, they provide an underground network many times larger than the aerial extent of the tree crowns. It is a characteristic that appears to give red pine both a resilience and responsiveness to a wide array of stand manipulations that cannot be explained adequately by crown processes alone.

Summary

In this Chapter we explore the consequences of several useful silvicultural practices and raise questions about the importance of below-ground processes.

- Row thinning compared to uniformly thinned plantations displays little or no difference in stand growth rates when both are thinned to the same residual stand densities.

- Intensity of thinning accounts for almost no stand growth when effects of age, SI, and stand density are removed.

- Individual tree-diameter variability, presumably a measure of uniformity of growing space, accounts for almost no stand growth after the effects of age, SI, and stand density have been removed.

- Below-ground processes suggest that biological activities in rooting zones contribute strongly to stand responsiveness in red pine.

Chapter 9. Exploring Silvicultural Options

Let us introduce by way of three examples some important managerial questions that can be examined based on the findings reported here, assisted by RP2005. Beyond these examples, users will be able to simulate a variety of red pine silvicultural and economic scenarios tailored to their individual land management goals, most of which will be far more complex than those examined here.

Estimating Stand Yields

Growth and yield comparisons can be made in response to a variety of management options and site qualities. These may start at age zero or at any intermediate age. To illustrate (fig. 24), let us explore the 100-year yield consequences of a middle-of-the-road thinning strategy for a broad range of SIs (40, 50, 60, 70, and 80, all starting with 800 established trees/acre, thinned to 120 ft²/acre at 10-year intervals beginning at age 30).

The importance of site quality to stand productivity is the most obvious consequence illustrated in this display. At age 100, the cumulative yield for each 10-foot increase in site class results in a volume gain of 2,600-2,700 ft³/acre. Stated another way, SI 70 land is more than twice as productive as SI 40 land. The benefits of better sites go beyond volume production. For example, the QMD at age 100 for SI 40 to SI 80 land will range,

---

Figure 24. *Cumulative net cubic-foot volume yields over a 100-year rotation in relation to a range of SIs, with similar thinning regimes for all sites.*

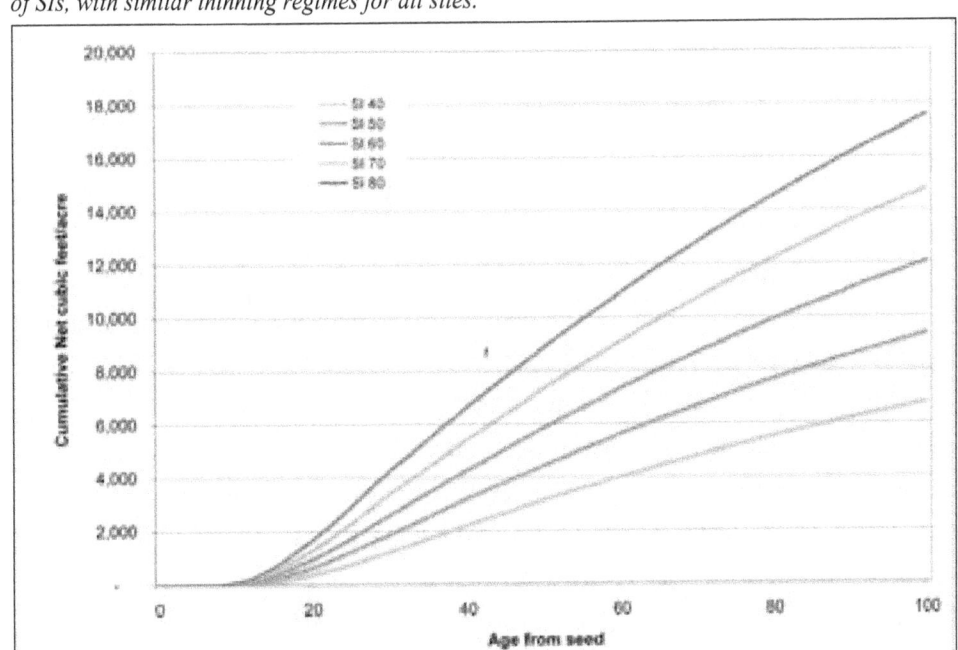

respectively, from 11.8, 13.7, 15.3, 16.6, to 17.7 inches. The 100-year board-foot yields range from 25 MBF on SI 40 land to nearly 80 MBF on SI 80 land. (SI 80 is outside our database but has been reported by others, hence its inclusion in this example). In terms of physical production, the importance of SI outweighs many other silvicultural considerations available to users.

The down side of better sites is higher establishment and management costs due to control of unwanted vegetation (see SI discussions in Chapter 3). The financial aspects of SI can be examined in RP2005. Still, with improved and lower-cost technologies (i.e., prescribed fire), better sites remain an attractive target for red pine investments.

Keep in mind that an analysis of this kind can begin and end at almost any stand age, and with an almost infinite combination of thinning regimes and financial assumptions.

PAI and MAI

Periodic Annual Increment (PAI) and Mean Annual Increment (MAI) are among the most useful characterizations of stand behavior in relation to a variety of management regimes. They are the biological equivalents of marginal and average cost curves in economic analysis. PAI tracks marginal rates of annual stand growth, peaking for red pine in the age range of 15 to 40 or later, depending on whether the units of measure are BA, cubic feet, or any of a variety of merchantability criteria. MAI, or average annual growth, represents the accumulation from age zero of standing volume, *plus thinning volumes, if any*, by stand age. As a caution, MAI is not meaningful unless stand yields can be reconstructed back to age zero. The culmination of MAI occurs where the PAI and MAI curves intersect and represents the rotation age that maximizes physical production for the product in question. The culmination of MAI may range in age from the 20s for BA growth to more than 100 years for sawtimber.

Figure 25 displays net PAI and MAI (ft³/acre/year) for three identical thinning regimes on SI 45, 60, and 75 land, all projected to stand age 150. The sawtooth-like appearance of the PAI curves emphasizes that thinning in vigorously growing young stands modifies stand density enough to significantly affect volume growth rate. Similar displays could be derived from RP2005 for a variety of thinning regimes, site indices, and merchantability standards, with substantially different curves.

These PAI/MAI relationships reinforce the importance of SI in productivity. They also tell us something about the age at which maximum PAI and MAI growth occurs. Also notice, for cubic feet at least, that SI has little influence on the age at which culmination occurs—in the late 20s for PAI and late 60s and early 70s for MAI. For other utilization standards (especially sawtimber) these relationships will occur at older ages and exhibit more variation.

Figure 25. *PAI and MAI in net ft³/acre projected to age 150 for SI 45, 60, and 75 land, starting with 1,200 established trees/acre, and thinned to 120 ft² at age 30 and 10-year intervals thereafter.*

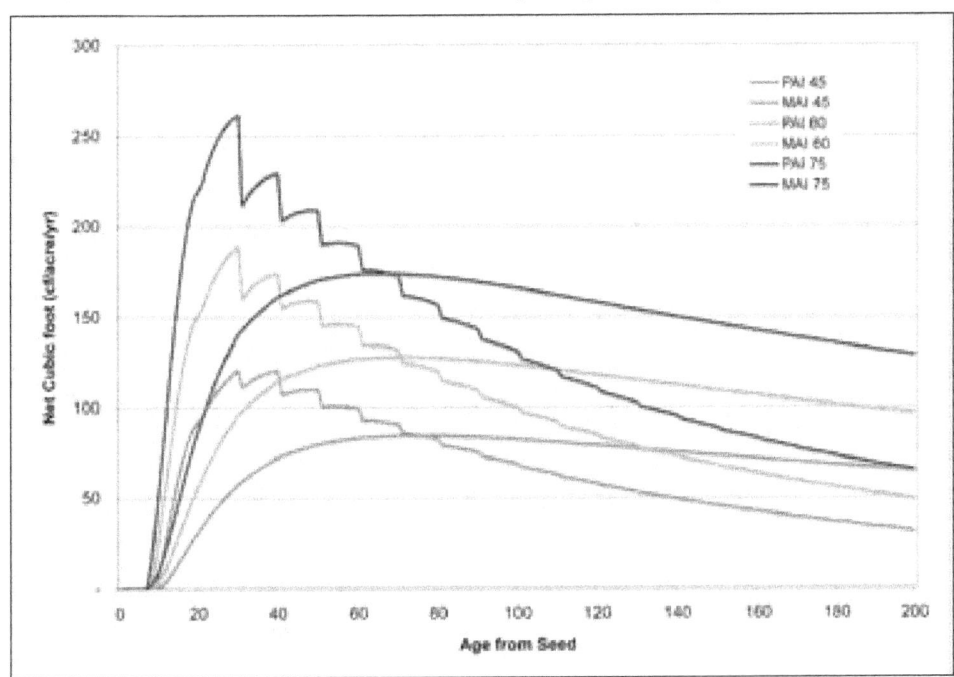

Another important question that can be addressed in part by a PAI/MAI analysis is the consequences of extended rotations, whether on public or private land. Notice in figure 18 the slow decline of PAI past its culmination, suggesting that red pine stands remains productive well into their second century. In addition, individual trees will increase in size and value with these long rotations. For example, with the thinning schedules used in this example, we could expect the QMD of the average tree at age 200 would be 19, 24, and 27 inches on SI 45, 60, and 75 land, respectively. In any event, in managed stands, where an economic premium is placed on larger trees, or where aesthetic considerations are high, extended rotations may be preferred. One can assess the biological and economic pluses and minuses of these longer rotations against various management goals and financial considerations.

Short-rotation Management

Still other managerial questions we might explore concern high yields, and, for red pine at least, short rotations These questions would focus on rapid stand growth at young ages and the effects of stand densities on yields (see Chapter 3, p 15, fig. 26). We also introduce in this section the ability of RP2005 to touch on the complex issues involved in financial analysis.

Figure 26. *Plot 99 seed source/growth monitoring study at stand age 26 on the Chippewa National Forest. In 59 years this SI 70 stand had a net yield of 88 cords/acre (4-inch top diameter), or a total stem volume yield of 9,160 ft³/acre. It has been thinned 9 times to provide growing space for the various seed sources (no statistical differences among sources) Erickson (2000).*

Let us illustrate in table 3 the consequences of short-rotation/high-density management with a simple example. We propose four thinning regimes on high site (SI 70) land, ranging from very low density (200 initial trees, thinned to 60 ft²/acre) to high density (1,200 initial trees, thinned to 160 ft²/acre). Thinning occurs at age 30 and 40 years during a 50-year rotation.

The cumulative yield at age 50 for the 200/60, 400/80, and 800/120 management options increases about 1,100 ft³/acre for each stepup in density, indicating the volume gains associated with higher densities. It is when we reach the 1,200/160 option that volume accumulation slows, increasing about 600 ft³/acre over the next lower density. Still, the difference in 50-year yields from highest to lowest density is nearly 3,000 ft³/acre. But notice also that volume harvested in thinning at ages 30 and 40 differs little among the four density regimes—a consequence that plays a substantial role in financial analyses.

In the same order shown in table 3, average tree diameters (QMD) at age 50 are 18.5, 13.9, 9.6, and 7.6 inches, indicating another set of possible trade-offs, this time favoring lower densities if early sawtimber production is the goal. And many other variations of density/age/SI alternatives could be considered.

What does this suggest for the silviculture of young stand management? Obviously, increased fiber yields, perhaps by 10 to 25 percent or more depending on strategies,

Table 3. *Fifty-year net yield (ft³/acre) in relation to four stand density thinning regimes (SI 70).*

| Mgt Option | Thinning – Age 30 | | | Thinning – Age 40 | | | Rotation – Age 50 | | |
| | Volume – CF | | QMD (in) | Volume – CF | | QMD (in) | Volume – CF | | QMD (in) |
	Before Thinning	Removed		Before Thinning	Removed		Final Harvest	Cumulative Yield	
200/60	2,015	947	10.2	2,709	1,295	14.2	2,944	5,186	18.5
400/80	2,746	1,322	8.4	3,242	1,357	11.1	3,583	6,262	13.9
800/120	3,434	1,298	6.7	4,187	1,358	8.2	4,739	7,395	9.6
1200/160	3,770	922	5.7	5,059	1,288	6.7	5,816	8,026	7.6

are possible by tilting toward higher stand densities. There will be substantial tradeoffs between the sizes and numbers of trees among the various options. One could also consider a high-density/short-rotation option that involves little or no thinning in order to obtain high biomass while eliminating cost of thinning. And there are wood quality questions to be weighed—such as branch size, wood density, and radial growth rates— that can be influenced by stand management practices during these early and dynamic years of stand growth.

Let us add to this complexity by examining some of the financial consequences of these short-rotation scenarios (table 4). We make two stipulations: (1) maintain constant costs per unit volume (material to be used for paper or reconstituted wood products) for operational activities (fall, buck, yard, load, haul, and harvest taxes), and administration functions (roads, taxes, administration costs), and (2) maintain constant prices for the volume harvested and incidental income. Since thinning (at ages 30 and 40) and rotation ages were the same for all options, the timing (but not quantity) of cash flow was also the same. The only variation among management options is volume (or fiber) yield. Costs applied to scenarios were gathered from information provided by current field managers and by Kilgore and Martin (2002).

Table 4. *Financial analysis of the four management options using constant cost and price assumptions. The net present value is presented at five different discount rates.*

| Mgt Option | Net Present Value | | | | | Return on Investment (ROI) |
	2.00%	3.00%	4.00%	5.00%	6.00%	
200/60	$16,922	$8,151	$1,763	$-3,006	$-6,638	4.34%
400/80	$17,129	$8,290	$1,860	$-2,935	$-6,584	4.35%
800/120	$17,385	$8,454	$1,973	$-2,853	$-6,523	4.37%
1200/160	$17,562	$8,561	$2,044	$-2,802	$-6,484	4.39%

Although each management option results in a different stand structure due to stand density and intensity of thinning, the financial returns are remarkably similar. We can better understand the dynamics of these outcomes by looking at thinning yields (table 3). They differ among options by no more than 200 ft^3/acre for the first thinning and 35 ft^3 for the second. The two factors that most influence financial returns are (1) initial expenditures, and (2) length of time for returns. Since the volume yields for the two thinnings (age 30 and 40) were approximately the same among options, we should expect our returns (ROIs) to be similar. In fact they are, ranging from 4.34 percent for the lowest density to 4.39 percent for the highest.

The main difference among management options occurs at the rotation age. The high-density stand produced 5,816 ft^3/acre at age 50, while the low-density option produced 2,944 ft^3/acre, about half, at the same age. However, since this income occurs 50 years after stand establishment, discounting largely eliminates economic gain from higher density options.

One may conclude that to maximize financial returns, stands should be kept at high densities and thinned heavily and early, or not thinned at all, but still with shorter rotations. If the goal is simply to produce fiber products, then these may be the best options. However, if the goal also includes other products (such as sawtimber or poles), or amenities such as wildlife, watershed protection, or aesthetics, then further analysis is required to better estimate income gained or foregone by longer rotations.

Chapter 10. Model Testing and Error Estimation

Data Limitations and Error Estimation

In mensurational terms, the datasets, both active and retired, are of high quality because of careful workmanship in plot layout, tree measurement techniques, and treatment applications. However, the 31 studies and growth plots differ widely in objectives and details of design and measurement interval. Thus, an essential and time-consuming part of this study was to reduce the large amount of information to a standardized format and set of data protocols for later analysis (Appendix I).

In statistical terms, there are many uncertainties about error and parameter estimation. Our aim was to extract as much information as we could from a large but statistically imperfect dataset. We touch on these questions at several points in the text and in Appendix III by the use of statistical indicators (R^2, various statistical tests), but urge reader caution in their interpretation because of the presence of serial and spatial correlation among observations (meaning that individual observations do not contribute as much information as they might if they were truly independent, and may introduce biases to some unknown extent).

In the end, we use standard statistical procedures modified by *a priori* knowledge of red pine growth behavior to create the growth models. We also frequently relied on simple graphic and numerical analysis to test the reasonableness of various relationships. We also elaborate at various places in the text and in Appendix III on the reasoning behind these relationships and on questions of risk and uncertainty. We encourage the reader to examine several graphs (figs. 5, 6, and 12) to gain, admittedly subjectively, some impression of how well the many observations fit the various growth prediction equations.

By way of conclusion, we test prediction equations against independent datasets as Lundgren (1983) did with earlier work.

Comparisons with Independent Data Sources

Some eight red pine datasets enabled us to compare independent stand growth estimates with those predicted from RP2005. For these comparisons, we emphasize BA growth, the principal driving component in model building and the one we can reconstruct most reliably from independent data sources.

We divided the datasets into two groups (table 3), the first derived from long-term field experiments that include a variety of thinning regimes. In many respects this population is similar to the one from which our BA model was constructed, that is extensive and uniform planted and natural stands on which replicated treatments of various kinds can be followed through time. It also represents an older age group that in turn relies most heavily on the BA portion of the combined growth model, and in which we have somewhat greater confidence than the TPA portion. This population, because of its uniformity and long-term care, represents the most favorable conditions for red pine stand growth in the Lake States.

The second group of data was collected for a variety of purposes from temporary plots broadly representing planted stands across the Lake States. These are the kinds of stands that users are likely to encounter at the first commercial thinning. The stands, up to 50 years of age, were unthinned with, presumably, uniformly distributed trees. Otherwise, stand histories are largely unknown. Growth predictions for this group rely heavily on the TPA portion of the combined growth model, the sector that was most difficult for growth forecasting.

For the first group of data, figure 27 displays predicted versus observed BA accumulated over the 20- to 38-year span of the four long-term experiments. Observations lying on the 45-degree line would represent full agreement between predicted and observed values. The superimposed regression line characterizes the predicted trend of the 38 observations in the four studies. If we average the predicted and the observed values, RP2005 overestimates BA growth for these four long-term studies by only about 0.8 percent.

Table 5. *Independent studies used to compare predicted versus observed BA growth (ft²/acre).*

Study	Location	Stand Age	Site Index	Number of observations
Long-term studies				
Hiawatha NF (Day, Rudolph 1972), (Rudolph et al. 1984)	Mich	27-47	~60	16[1]
Dunbar (Day, Rudolph 1971), (Rudolph et al.1984)	Mich	28-56	~70	6[1]
Kellog (Rudolph et al. 1984)				
Cutfoot prescribed burning Buckman	Mich	26-46	~65	9[1]
(Unpublished)	Minn	89-130	~50	7[1]
Temporary plots				
Alban (Unpublished)	Mich, Wis, Minn	30-40	36-75	6
Alban (1984)	Minn	48-52	62-68	5
Alban (1988)	Mich, Wis, Minn	22-52	40-74	25
Hannah (1969)	Mich	27-54	38-80	15

[1] Each observation represents the mean value of a treatment, each containing 3-4 replications.

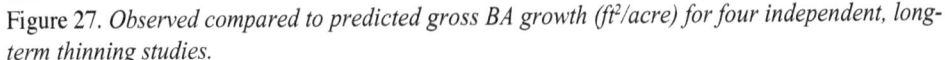

Figure 27. *Observed compared to predicted gross BA growth (ft²/acre) for four independent, long-term thinning studies.*

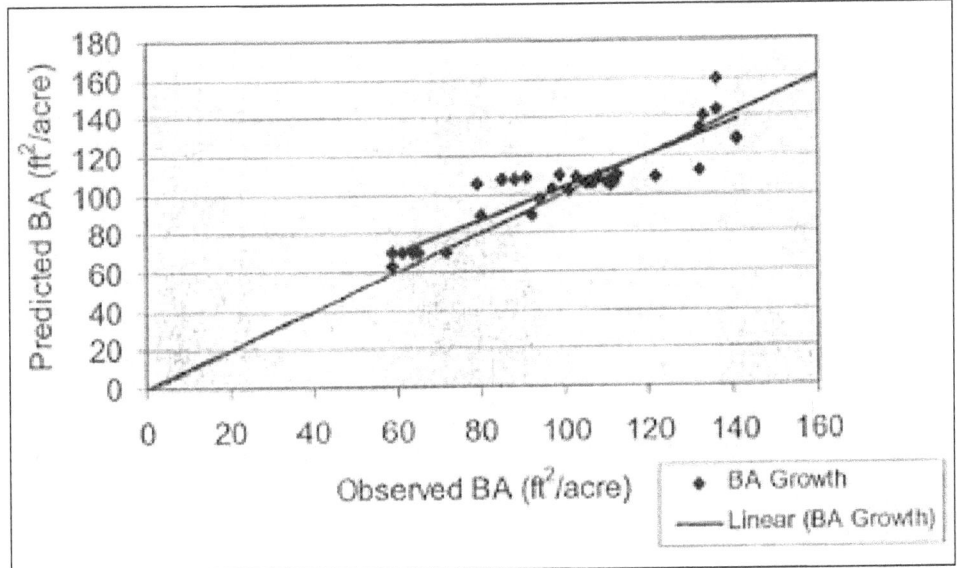

For the second group of data, figure 28 displays the dispersion of observed versus predicted values, including a regression line fitted to the observations. Here we see greater departure from the 45-degree line, and tendencies for predicted growth to be greater than actual growth, more so at lower than at high values. In terms of averages for this dataset, predicted BA growth is 12.2 percent greater than observed growth.

Figure 28. *Observed versus predicted gross BA (ft²/acre) for 51 unthinned temporary sample plots.*

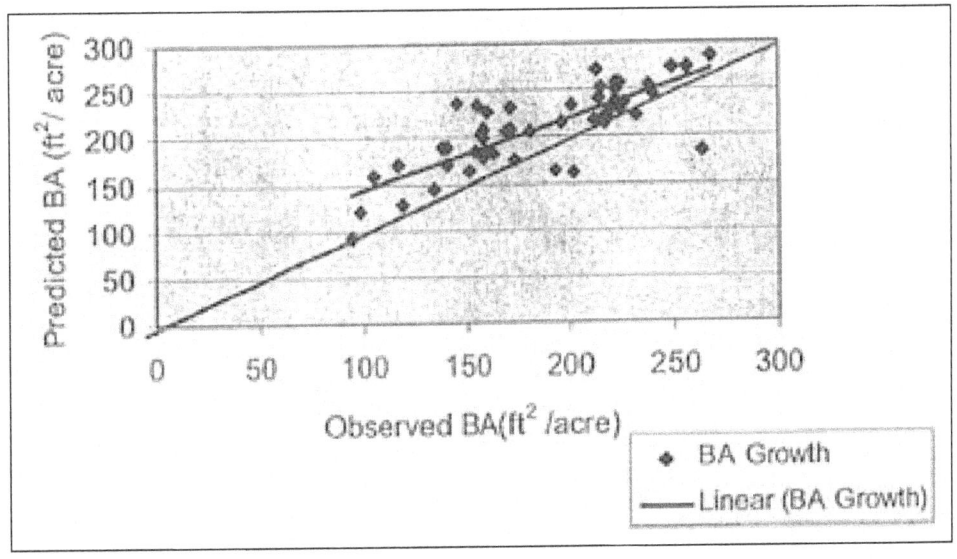

Summary

What can we conclude when comparing growth estimates from RP2005 with observed growth from independent sets of data? The comparisons with the four long-term studies suggest that our model predicts BA growth reasonably well, overestimating BA growth by less than 1 percent. We need to repeat that this dataset approximates the kind of stands from which the models were constructed.

Comparisons with the 51 temporary plots tend to overestimate observed growth by about 12 percent. The history of these stands is far more uncertain than that in the first group, and, depending on local experience, a user may want to use the provisions available in RP2005 to adjust growth estimates for large and irregular stands.

There is some suggestion from the regression lines in the long-term studies, and a more pronounced one in the temporary plots, of overestimation of growth rates in young, low-density stands. This is a complexity of model-building about which we were aware but could not completely overcome.

Two points need emphasis. The small measurement plots and relatively uniform stands in which most research studies are installed invariably yield overestimates of growth responses in larger and more variable tracts. Growth estimates must be tailored to the specific conditions encountered by users. RP2005 allows the user to insert at the input tab an adjustment factor to account for these discrepancies.

The second point is that our growth model is more sensitive to the prescriptive or diagnostic aspects of stand management than it is at estimating growth responses on larger tracts. These diagnostic aspects include such questions as optimum density levels, how many trees to plant, the consequences of site quality, what rotation age, which thinning method, and many others. In addition to the adjustment procedures available in RP2005, we have attempted to provide sufficient information in Appendix III for skilled programmers to modify or substitute growth equations that better capture specific forest conditions.

Literature Cited

Alban, David H. 1978. Growth of adjacent red and jack pine plantations in the Lake States. Journal of Forestry. 76(7): 418-421.

Alban, David H. 1979. Estimating site potential from the early height growth of red pine in the Lake States. Res. Pap. NC-166. St. Paul, MN: U.S. Department of Agriculture, Forest Service, North Central Forest Experiment Station. 7 p.

Alban, David H. 1984. Red pine site evaluation based on tree growth and soils. In: Marty, Robert, ed. Managing red pine, proceedings of the SAF Region 5 technical conference; 1984 October 1-3; Marquette, MI. SAF Publ. 85-02. Bethesda, MD: Society of American Foresters: 79-100.

Alban, David H. 1985. Volume comparison of pine, spruce, and aspen growing side by side. Res. Note NC-327. St. Paul, MN: U.S. Department of Agriculture, Forest Service, North Central Forest Experiment Station. 6 p.

Alban, David H. 1988. Nutrient accumulation in planted red and jack pine. Res. Pap. NC-282. St. Paul MN: U.S. Department of Agriculture, Forest Service, North Central Forest Experiment Station. 6 p.

Alban, David H.; Prettyman, Donald H. 1984. Height growth of red pine on fine-textured soils. Res. Pap. NC-249. St. Paul, MN: U.S. Department of Agriculture, Forest Service, North Central Forest Experiment Station. 6 p.

Anderson, Paul D.; et al. 2002. Thinning in mature eastern white pine: 43-year case study. The Forestry Chronicle. 78(4): 539-549.

Bailey, Robert L.; Ware, Kenneth D. 1983. Compatible basal-area growth and yield model for thinned and unthinned stands. Canadian Journal of Forest Research. 13: 563-571.

Belcher, David W.; Holdaway, Margaret R.; Brand, Gary J. 1982. A description of STEMS: the stand and tree evaluation and modeling system. Gen. Tech. Rep. NC-79. St. Paul, MN: U.S. Department of Agriculture, Forest Service, North Central Forest Experiment Station. 18 p.

Benzie, John W. 1977. Manager's handbook for red pine in the North Central states. Gen. Tech. Rep. NC-33. St. Paul, MN: U.S. Department of Agriculture, Forest Service, North Central Forest Experiment Station. 22 p.

Benzie, John W.; McCumber, James E. 1983. Red pine. In: Burns, R.M., tech. comp. Silvicultural systems for the major forest types of the United States. Agric. Handb. 445. Washington, DC: U.S. Department of Agriculture, Forest Service: 89-91.

Bottenfield, Timothy R.; Reed, David D. 1988. Estimating site quality of young red pine plantations by growth intercept methods. Northern Journal of Applied Forestry. 5: 91-93.

Bowyer, Jim L. 2002. Red pine utilization and markets. In: Gilmore, D.W.; Yount, L.S., eds. Proceedings of the red pine SAF Region 5 technical conference. Staff Pap. Ser. 157. St. Paul, MN: University of Minnesota, Forest Resources Department, College of Natural Resources; 124-130.

Bowyer, Jim L.; Shmulsky, Rubin; Haygreen, John G. 2003. Sivicultural practices and wood quality chapter 12. In: Forest products and wood science–an introduction. [Ames, IA]: Iowa State University Press. 554 p.

Brand, David G.; Magnussen, S. 1988. Asymmetric, two-sided competition in even-aged monocultures of red pine. Canadian Journal of Forest Research. 18(7): 901-910.

Buchman, Roland G. 1979. Mortality functions. In: A generalized forest growth projection system applied to the Lake States region. Gen. Tech. Rep. NC-49. St. Paul, MN: U.S. Department of Agriculture, Forest Service, North Central Forest Experiment Station: 47-55.

Buchman, Roland G. 1983. Survival predictions for major Lake States tree species. Res. Pap. NC-233. St. Paul, MN: U.S. Department of Agriculture, Forest Service, North Central Forest Experiment Station. 7 p.

Buckman, Robert E. 1961. Development and use of three stand volume equations for Minnesota. Journal of Forestry. 59(8): 573-575.

Buckman, Robert E. 1962a Growth and yield of red pine in Minnesota. Tech. Bull. 1272. Washington, DC: U.S. Department of Agriculture. 50 p.

Buckman, Robert E. 1962b. Three growing-stock density experiments in Minnesota red pine: a progress report. Sta. Pap. 99. St. Paul, MN: U.S. Department of Agriculture, Forest Service, Lake States Forest Experiment Station. 10 p.

Buckman, Robert E.; Lundgren, Allen. 1962. Three pine release experiments in northern plantation. Tech. Note 533. St. Paul, MN: U.S. Department of Agriculture, Forest Service, Lake States Forest Experiment Station. 2 p.

Buckman, Robert E.; Wambach, Robert F. 1966. Physical responses and economic implications of thinning methods in red pine. [Bethesda, MD]: Society of American Foresters Proceedings, 1965: 185-189.

Byrne, J.C.; Reed, D.D. 1985. Complex compatible taper and volume estimation systems for red and loblolly pine. Forest Science. 32: 423-443.

Byrnes, W.R.; Bramble, W.C. 1955. Growth and yield of plantation-grown red pine at various spacings. Journal of Forestry. 53(8): 562-565.

Carmean, Willard H.; Thrower, James S. 1995. Early height growth and site index for planted red pine in North Central Ontario. Northern Journal of Applied Forestry. 12(1): 23-29.

Chapman, H.H. 1946. Origin and results of the seed-tree experiment with Norway pine on the Chippewa National Forest. Journal of Forestry. 44: 178-183.

Cooley, John H. 1969. Initial thinning in red pine plantations. Res. Pap. NC-35. St. Paul, MN: U.S. Department of Agriculture, Forest Service, North Central Forest Experiment Station. 6 p.

Curtis, Robert O. 1970. Stand density measures: an interpretation. Forest Science. 16: 403-414.

Davis, Lawrence S.; Johnson, K. Norman. 1987. Forest management. 3d ed. [New York, NY]: McGraw-Hill, Inc. 790 p.

Day, M.W. 1941. The root system of red pine saplings. Journal of Forestry. 39: 468-472.

Day, M.W.; Bey, C.F.; Rudolph, V.J. 1960. Site index for planted red pine by the 5-year growth intercept method. Journal of Forestry. 58(3): 198-202.

Day, M.W.; Rudolph, V.J. 1966. Early growth results of thinning plantation red pine by three methods. Michigan Agricultural Experiment Station Quarterly Bulletin. 49(2): 183-188.

Day, M.W.; Rudolph, V.J. 1972. Thinning plantation red pine. Res. Rep. 151. East Lansing, MI: Michigan State University, Agriculture Experiment Station. 10 p.

Erickson, Glen W. 1996. Growth and yield of a 59-year-old red pine plantation (Plot 99) in northern Minnesota. Res. Note NC-369. St. Paul, MN: U.S. Department of Agriculture, Forest Service, North Central Forest Experiment Station. 8 p.

Eyre, F.H.; Zehngraff, Paul. 1948. Red pine management in Minnesota. Circ. 778. Washington, DC: U.S. Department of Agriculture.

Frederick, D.J.; Coffman, M.S. 1978. Red pine plantation biomass exceeds sugar maple on northern hardwood sites. Journal of Forestry. 76: 13-15.

Gartner, Barbara L. 2005. Assessing wood characteristics and wood quality in intensively managed plantations. Journal of Forestry. 103(2): 75-77.

Gevorkiantz, S.R.; Rudolph, P.O.; Zehngraff, P.J. 1943 A tree classification for aspen, jack pine and second growth red pine. Journal of Forestry. 41: 268-274.

Gevorkiantz, S.R. 1957. Site index curves for red pine in the Lake States. Tech. Notes 484. St. Paul, MN: U.S. Department of Agriculture, Forest Service, Lake States Forest Experiment Station. 2 p.

Gevorkiantz, S.R.; Olsen, L.P. 1955. Composite volume tables for timber and their application in the Lake States. Tech. Bull. 1104. Washington, DC: U.S. Department of Agriculture. 51 p.

Gregory, G.R. 1987. Resource economics for foresters. [New York, NY]: John Wiley & Sons. 477 p.

Gunter, J.E.; Rudolph, V.J. 1968. Economics of red pine release on the Fife Lake state forest. Michigan Agricultural Experiment Station Quarterly Bulletin. 50(4): 507-519.

Hahn, J.T. 1981. Tree volume and biomass equations for the Lake States. Res. Pap. NC-250. St. Paul, MN: U.S. Department of Agriculture, Forest Service, North Central Forest Experiment Station. 10 p.

Hannah, Peter R. 1969. Stemwood production related to soils in Michigan red pine plantations. Forest Science. 15(3): 320-326.

Harms, Jan C.; et al. 1990. Market assessment and economic potential of the red pine utility pole industry in Wisconsin. Northern Journal of Applied Forestry. 7(4): 189-193.

Hyldahl, Carol A.; Grossman, Gerald H. 1993. User's guide: RPGrow$: red pine growth and analysis spreadsheet for the Lake States. Gen. Tech. Rep. NC-156. St. Paul, MN: U.S. Department of Agriculture, Forest Service, North Central Forest Experiment Station. 27 p.

Jozsa, L.A.; Middleton, G.R. 1994. A discussion of wood quality attributes and their practical implications. Spec. Publ. SP-34. Vancouver, BC: Forintek Canada Corp., Western Laboratory.

Kilgore, Michael; Martin, Katherine. 2002. The economic of red pine management in the Lake States. In: Gilmore, D.W.; Yount, L.S., eds. Proceedings of the Red Pine SAF Region 5 technical conference. Staff Pap. Ser. 157. St. Paul, MN: University of Minnesota, College of Natural Resources, Department of Forest Resources: 112-123.

Laidly, Paul R.; Barse, Robert G. 1979. Spacing affects knot surface in red pine plantations. Res. Note NC-246. St. Paul, MN: U.S. Department of Agriculture, Forest Service, North Central Forest Experiment Station. 3 p.

Larocque, G.R. 1995. Wood relative density development in red pine (*Pinus resinosa* Ait.) stands as affected by different initial spacings. Forest Science. 41(4): 709-728.

Larocque, Guy R.; Marshall, Peter L. 1994. Crown development in red pine stands. II: relationships with stem growth. Canadian Journal of Forest Research. 24(4): 775-784.

Larson, Philip R. 1963. Stem form development of forest trees. For. Sci. Monogr. 5. Washington, DC: Society of American Foresters. 42 p.

Lundgren, Allen L. 1981. The effect of initial number of trees per acre and thinning densities on timber yields from red pine plantations in the Lake States. Res. Pap. NC-193. St. Paul, MN: U.S. Department of Agriculture, Forest Service, North Central Forest Experiment Station. 25 p.

Lundgren, Allen L. 1982. Can red pine in the Lake States out produce loblolly and slash pine in the South? In: Artificial regeneration of conifers in the Upper Great Lakes region. Houghton, MI: Michigan Technological University: 337-344.

Lundgren, Allen L. 1983. New site productivity estimates for red pine in the Lake States. Journal of Forestry. 81(11): 714-717.

Lundgren, Allen L. 1985. REDPINE - a growth and yield simulation model. In: Marty, Robert, ed. Managing red pine, proceedings of the SAF Region 5 technical conference; 1984 October 1-3; Marquette, MI. SAF Publ. 85-02. Bethesda, MD: Society of American Foresters: 185-203.

Lundgren, Allen L.; Dolid, William A. 1970. Biological growth functions describe published site index curves for Lake States timber species. Res. Pap. NC-36. St. Paul, MN: U.S. Department of Agriculture, Forest Service, North Central Forest Experiment Station. 9 p.

Mack, T.J.; Burk, T.E. 2002. Application of a density management diagram for Lake States red pine management. In: Gilmore, D.W.; Yount, L.S., eds. Proceedings of the red pine SAF Region 5 technical conference. Staff Pap. Ser. 157. St. Paul, MN: University of Minnesota, College of Natural Resources, Department of Forest Resources: 90-95.

Maeglin, Robert R. 1967. Effect of tree spacing on weight yields for red pine and jack pine. Journal of Forestry. 65: 647-650.

Magnussen, S.; Brand, D.G. 1989. A competition process driven model for red pine. Inf. Rep. PI-X-89. Chalk River, Ontario: Petawawa National Forestry Institute. 38 p.

Newnham, R.M. 1988. A variable form taper function. Inf. Rep. PI-X-83. Chalk River, Ontario: Petawawa National Forestry Institute, Forestry Canada. 33 p.

Pyhrr, S.A.; Cooper, J.R. 1982. Real estate investment—strategy, analysis, decisions. [New York, NY]: John Wiley & Sons. 477 p.

Read, David J. 1997. Mycorrhizal fungi: the ties that bind. Nature. 338: 517-518.

Rudolf, P.O. 1990. Red pine. In: Burns, R.M.; Honkala, B.H., eds. Silvics of North America. Volume 1. Conifers. Agric. Handb. 654. Washington, DC: U.S. Department of Agriculture, Forest Service: 442-455.

Rudolph, Victor J.; Day, Maurice W.; Lemmien, Walter A.; et al. 1984. Thinning planted red pine in Michigan. Res. Rep. 461. East Lansing, MI: Michigan State University, Agricultural Experiment Station. 18 p.

Schlaegel, Bryce E. 1975. Yields of four 40-year-old conifers and aspen in adjacent stands. Canadian Journal of Forest Research. 5(2): 278-280.

Schmidt, Thomas L. 2002. Red pine in the Northern Lake States. In: Gilmore, D.W.; Yount, L.S., eds. Proceeding of the SAF Region 5 technical conference. Staff Pap. Ser. 157. St. Paul, MN: University of Minnesota, Forest Resources Department, College of Natural Resources: 3-16.

Simard, Susanne W.; et.al. 1997. Net transfer of carbon between ectomycorrhizal tree species in the field. Nature. 388: 579-582.

Smith, David M. 2003. Effect of method of thinning on wood production in a red pine plantation. Northern Journal of Applied Forestry. 20(1): 39-42.

Smith, D.J.; Woods, M.E. 1997. Red pine and white pine density management diagrams for Ontario. South Central Science Sections Tech. Rep. 48. North Bay, ON: Ontario Ministry of Natural Resources. 31 p.

Smith, N.J.; Hann, D.W. 1986. A growth model based on the self-thinning rule. Canadian Journal of Forest Research. 16: 330-334.

Smith, S.E.; Read, D.J. 1997. Mycorrhizal symbiosis. 2d ed. London: Academic Press. 605 p.

Snellgrove, Thomas A.; et al., eds. 1984. User's guide for cubic measurement. U.S. Department of Agriculture, Forest Service, Pacific Northwest Research Station and the University of Washington, College of Forest Resources Contribution 52. 107 p.

Spurr, Stephen H. 1952. Forest inventory. New York, NY: The Ronald Press Company. 476 p.

Stiell, W.M. 1966. Red pine crown development in relation to spacing. Publ. 1145. Ottawa, Ontario: Canada Department of Forestry. 44 p.

Stiell, W.M. 1970. Some competitive relations in a red pine plantation. Publ.1275. [Ottawa, Ontario]: Department of Fisheries and Forestry, Canadian Forestry Service. 10 p.

Stiell, W.M. 1982. Growth of clumped vs. equally spaced trees. Forestry Chronicle. 58(1): 23-25.

Stiell, W.M. 1984. The Petawawa red pine plantation trials. In: Marty, Robert, ed. Managing red pine: proceedings of the second Region 5 technical conference; 1984 October 1-3; Marquette, MI. SAF Publ. 85-02. Bethesda, MD: Society of American Foresters: 204-215.

Stiell, W.M.; Berry, A.B. 1977. A 20-year trial of red pine planted at seven spacings. Inf. Rep. FMR-X-97. Ottawa, Ontario: Department of the Environment, Canadian Forestry Service, Forest Management Institute. 25 p.

Stone, D.M. 1976. Growth of red pine (*Pinus resinosa*) planted on a northern hardwood site. Res. Note NC-210. St. Paul, MN: U.S. Department of Agriculture, Forest Service, North Central Forest Experiment Station. 4 p.

USDA-Forest Service. 1999. Wood handbook: wood as an engineering material. Gen. Tech. Rep. FPL-GTR-113. Madison, WI: U.S. Department of Agriculture, Forest Service, Forest Products Laboratory.

Wambach, Robert F. 1967. A silvicultural and economic appraisal of initial spacing in red pine. Minneapolis, MN: University of Minnesota. 282 p. Ph.D. dissertation.

Woolsey, Theodore S., Jr.; Chapman, Herman H. 1914. Norway pine in the Lake States. Bull. 139. Washington, DC: U.S. Department of Agriculture. 42 p.

Zeide, Boris. 1987. Analysis of the 3/2 power law of self thinning. Forest Science. 33(2): 517-537.

Zeide, Boris. 1991. Self-thinning and stand density. Forest Science. 37(2): 517-523.

Appendix I. Database and Protocols

The Datasets

The 31 datasets used in this analysis came from a variety of thinning studies and growth-monitoring plots, each differing in purpose, design, and location (table 4). The mensurational quality of the datasets is high, a result of careful plot layout, measurement techniques, and execution of assigned treatments. A major task, however, was to reduce the large database to standardized definitions and format.

Most pre-WWII studies are unreplicated; most post-WWII studies (except growth-monitoring plots) follow modern statistical procedures, including replication and randomized assignment of treatments. Most early studies have been retired; many of the later ones are still active. The statistically designed studies (i.e., stand density, tree spacing, thinning-methods studies) lend themselves to stand-alone analysis, reinforced, of course, by similar studies elsewhere. We use these individual studies to illustrate and address specific silvicultural questions.

For growth forecasting, each measurement plot and each sequential growth interval is treated as a separate observation, since each contained some information differing from its neighbors or from preceding measurements on the same plot. With this dataset we were able to generate 3,671 growth observations. This practice raises serious statistical questions of auto- or serial correlation. We touch on these questions and other data inadequacies in Chapter 10 on model testing.

Data Protocols

Individual measurement plots ranged in size from 1/10 acre to more than one acre—all were converted to a per-acre basis and weighted equally in analysis. All plots were surrounded by similarly treated buffer zones of various sizes. For the studies that had several measurement plots within the same treatment block, each plot measurement period is treated as a separate observation. Most experiments, however, had only a single measurement plot per replication.

Measurement intervals averaged about 5 years; some were as short as 1-3 years, others 10 years or longer. For several experiments, two short intervals (1-3 years) were combined. In a number of studies, measurements were made during the active growing season. The problem thus created could sometimes be avoided by combining two short measurement intervals when the in-between measurement was during the growing season. In other circumstances, the growing season measurement was assigned to the nearest dormant season to avoid working with fractional growing seasons.

In addition, the following protocols were adopted to further standardize the data sets:

- Stand age is defined as years from seed.
- Minimum tree diameters were 1.0 inches d.b.h.
- Plots with 25 percent or more of other species (i.e., jack pine, white pine, aspen), or with two or more age classes were rejected.
- Ingrowth (generally 1 percent or less in total BA) was ignored.
- Plots damaged by such activities as road construction, log landings, or excessive animal and storm damage were eliminated.
- Stand height and SI was recorded in a variety of ways among studies. See Chapter 3 on site quality for standardizing procedures.

All data from the 3,671 individual observations were reduced to a common data format that included:

- Stand and plot descriptors.
- Average annual gross and net stand BA growth and arithmetic and QMD diameter growth—the dependent or response variables.
- Age, SI, number of trees/acre, average tree diameter (arithmetic and QMD), amount and percent BA removed in thinning. **d/D** values (ratio of average tree diameter removed to average diameter left standing), and standard deviation of tree diameters—the independent or explanatory variables.

This large dataset in turn provided material for stand modeling and for analysis of such silvicultural questions as intensity of thinning, thinning methods, and effects of numbers of trees and structure on stand growth. Table 6 describes the 31 data sets and their purposes.

Table 6. *Experiments and growth plots used in growth and yield of Red Pine.*

Study Name and Location	Year of Stand Origin	Site Index	Year Study -- Started	Year Study -- Ended	Purpose[1]	Number of Plots[2]	Growth Periods[2]
1. Bena Plots 1-4 (Minn)	1820	47-52	1925	1979	SD, R	4	11
2. Plots 18-21 "Common Sense Plots" (Minn)	1870	48-51	1927	1954	SD	4	6
3. Plots 22-25 "Graveyard Plots" (Minn)	1905	45-49	1927	1952	PC	4	5
4. Birch Lake Plantation Release Study (Minn)	1913	59-67	1932	1956	RL	3	5
5. Longville Plots (Minn)	1896	58	1941	1955	GM	2	2
6. Marcell Plots 1-14 (Minn)	1800	54-64	1944	Active	GM	14	9
7. Lake 13 Plots (Minn)	1820	50-57	1945	Active	GM	11	9
8. Portage Lake Thinning Study (Minn)	1902	52-59	1947	Active	SD	15	9

Table 6. *Experiments and growth plots used in growth and yield of Red Pine (continued).*

Study Name and Location	Year of Stand Origin	Site Index	Year Study -- Started	Year Study -- Ended	Purpose[1]	Number of Plots[2]	Growth Periods[2]
9. Rommel Inventory Plots (Minn)	1905	54-57	1949	19156	GM	5	2
10. Cutting Cycles Study (Minn)							
3 Year Cycle	1870	44-52	1949	1955	TC	17	2
6 Year Cycle	1870	44-51	1949	1955	TC	6	1
11. Growing Stock Levels Study (80 yr) (Minn)	1870	45-56	1950-1951	Active	SD	45	9
12. Growing Stock Levels Study (40 yr) (Minn)	1905	44-51	1949	1960	SD	33	2
13. Plot 99 Growth Study (Minn)	1934	70	1951	Active	GM	1	9
14. Thinning Methods Study (Minn)	1870	44-53	1950-1953	Active	TM	90	8
15. Buck Creek Plantation I (Mich)	1915	36-49	1951	Active	SD	33	7
16. Buck Creek Plantation II (Mich)	1915	38	1953	1958	GM	1	1
17. Croton Dam Plantation Density Study (Mich)	1926	57-70	1952	Active	SD	23	8
Bosom Field Plantation Studies (Mich)							
18. Bosom I - Stand Density	1910	51-61	1951	Active	SD	21	7
19. Bosom II - Unthinned	1910	54-60	1934	Active	GM	3	7
20. Bosom III - Row Thinning	1910	52-63	1951	Active	RT	6	7
21. Bosom IV - Special Study	1910	62	1939	Active	GM	1	6
22. Bosom V - Pole Study	1910	56-68	1956	Active	GM	2	6
23. Bosom VI - Crown Thinning	1910	50	1955	Active	TM	3	6
24. MANDO Stand Density Study (Minn)	1899	51-59	1956-1957	1987	SD	18	6
25. Birch Lake Plantation Thinning Study (Minn)	1912-1913	49-69	1957	Active	SD, TM	54	6
26. Sooner Club Plantation (Mich)	1929	52-60	1960	Active	SD, TM, RT	46	5
27. Ravenna Plantation (Mich)	1932	50-66	1960	Active	SD, RT	38	5
28. Spooner Plantation Spacing Study (Wis)	1955	64-74	1958	1995	SD	36	5
29. Black River Falls Plantation Spacing Study (Wis)	1955	61-75	1958	1995	SD	30	5
30. Chapman Plantation (Minn)	1897	60-62	1930	Active	GM	3	13
31. Wambach Plantation Spacing Study[3]	Multiple	40-78	1959	1962	SD	55	1

[1] Study Purpose: SD, Stand Density; R, Regeneration; TM, Thinning Methods; RL, Release; PC, Precommercial Thinning; RT, Row Thinning; GM, Growth Monitoring.

[2] A number of plots and/or measurement periods within individual studies were eliminated because they failed to meet data protocols, thus reducing the total number of observations that otherwise would be available.

[3] The Wambach study consisted of 55 temporary unthinned plots in young plantations across the States of Mich., Wis., and Minn.

Appendix II

RP2005 Growth and Yield Models

RP2005 is the latest in a series of growth and yield forecasting models for even-aged red pine stands in the Lake States. Earlier versions were generally based on the growth and yield estimates of Buckman/Wambach/Lundgren.

As the main body of this report and Appendix I outline, the equations used in RP2005 were derived from a much larger database than earlier work, with a substantially revised set of underlying mathematical relationships (displayed in Appendix III). RP2005 can be downloaded on the Internet from the USFS North Central Research Station at the following URL address:

http://www.ncrs.fs.fed.us/library/

RP2005 was implemented as a spreadsheet application in Microsoft Excel™. There are both advantages and disadvantages to this approach. We chose Excel because it permitted us to represent a complex model in a user-friendly format. We expect that, as new information becomes available or as alternative programming languages offer advantages, users may want to modify RP2005 or substitute alternative programs (see below).

To run RP2005, you will need Microsoft Excel™ installed on your computer. Excel will run on either Macintosh or PC (Windows) computers.

Running RP2005

The RP2005 format contains several worksheets outlining required inputs and displaying various outputs. Two levels of instructions are provided, both intended to keep RP2005 user-friendly.

The first is a series of <u>mini-help statements</u> and cautions attached to the input requirements of the program. We hope this will be adequate for most users of RP2005. Additional hidden tabs provide more information for those who want to explore outputs in greater depth. The second is a <u>User Manual</u> located at the last tab of the program. This provides more detail on both the input requirements of RP2005 and its various outputs.

Modifying RP2005

Past experience with red pine growth and yield modeling suggests that RP2005 will require revision, for example, by substituting alternative growth estimators, using newer programming and graphic techniques, modifying assumptions, or correcting errors. Anticipating this, we have attempted to provide sufficient mathematical background in Appendix III that a skilled practitioner can modify RP2005 (generally with a new name), or employ other programming languages to capture features of modeling that are most meaningful to the user. We hope that these modifications could be made available to others, perhaps through the URL address above, or through the USDA, Forest Service, North Central Research Station.

In this regard, coauthor, Dr. T.J. Hanson, is preparing a version of the underlying growth model in REALbasic, tentatively labeled RPYld-06. This model will run on Windows, Macintosh, and Linux-based machines. The advantages of this model are that it does not require Excel software, can be run on multiple platforms and consumes less memory. The input and output formats are similar to the Excel version. We expect this program, including operating instructions, to be available at the above URL address.

Appendix III. The Mathematical Models Underlying the Red Pine Simulations

Notational Preliminaries

We frequently use Greek letters to denote parameters of our models. For readers not familiar with the Greek alphabet, here's a list of the Greek letters we use along with the English names of those letters: α = alpha, β = beta, γ = gamma, δ = delta, λ = lambda, μ = mu, σ = sigma, τ = tau, and ϕ = phi. The symbol "Δ" is a capital delta, and is often used in mathematics to signify the "change" in some quantity.

An alternative notation for the exponential function e^x is $\exp(x)$. This alternative notation is especially useful for readability when the exponent is an algebraic expression. For example, the expression

$$\exp\left[-\frac{(x-\mu)^2}{2\sigma^2}\right]$$

occurs in the definition of the "normal" distribution in statistics. The "natural" logarithm (i.e., the logarithm to the base e) is denoted $\ln(.)$. The symbol "$\equiv$" means "is identically equal to."

The Height Function and the Breakout Age

To establish notation, let

t = Age $\equiv$ the stand age (in years) from seed,

s = SI $\equiv$ the site index of the stand, and

$h(t)$ = the average height (in feet) of the dominant and co-dominant trees in a stand of red pine of age t. This is the "height" function.

Lundgren and Dolid (1970) fitted a height function of the form

$$h(t) = \alpha s\left(1 - e^{-\beta t}\right)^\gamma \tag{1}$$

(where α, β, and γ are coefficients) to tabular data compiled by Gevorkiantz (1957). They found that $\alpha = 1.890$, $\beta = 0.01979$, and $\gamma = 1.3892$.

The Lundgren-Dolid height function has two imperfections, one minor and the other significant. The minor imperfection is that $h(50)$ is not exactly equal to s as required by the definition of "site index"; instead, $h(50)$ is slightly smaller than s. To correct this imperfection, we refitted the Lundgren-Dolid equation to Gevorkiantz's data while enforcing the constraint that $h(50) = s$. This investigation yielded the following revised estimates of the coefficients: $\alpha = 1.8604$, $\beta = 0.020928$, and $\gamma = 1.4349$.

The significant imperfection concerns the height of stands of red pine at ages between 0 and 20 years. Gevorkiantz's tables only include heights of stands with ages between 20 and 120 years, and the Lundgren-Dolid height function fits these data beautifully. Although extensive data on the heights of stands younger than 20 years are not available, there is universal agreement among knowledgeable observers that the heights predicted by the Lundgren-Dolid height function are too large for these younger stands. To correct this imperfection, we examined a number of biologically plausible functional forms for a height function for "younger" stands, i.e., stands less than 20 years of age. We found that a younger stand height function of the form

$$h(t) = s\left(at^2 - bt^4\right) \tag{2}$$

can achieve satisfactory results when the coefficients a and b are cleverly chosen. A reasonable requirement on the younger stand height function is that the functions given by eqs. (1) and (2) join smoothly (without a discontinuity or corner) at $t = 20$. This requirement implies that $a = 1.41876 \times 10^{-3}$ and $b = 1.05304 \times 10^{-6}$. This height function yields heights at low ages that are consistent with observation.

In summary, the height function used in the red pine simulation is

$$h(t) = \begin{cases} \alpha s(1 - e^{-\beta t})^{\gamma} & \text{for } t \geq 20, \\ s(at^2 - bt^4) & \text{for } 0 \leq t \leq 20 \end{cases} \tag{3}$$

where $\alpha = 1.8604$, $\beta = 0.020928$, $\gamma = 1.4349$, $a = 1.41876 \times 10^{-3}$ and $b = 1.05304 \times 10^{-6}$. This height function[5] is shown in figure 7 of the text for several values of s.

The "breakout age" of a stand is defined as the age (from seed) when the stand first reaches "breast height" (i.e., 4.5 feet). For all stands of economic relevance, the breakout age will be earlier than 20 years. It follows from eq. (2) that the breakout age $\bar{t} = \bar{t}(s)$ satisfies

$$4.5 = s\left(a\bar{t}^2 - b\bar{t}^4\right). \tag{4}$$

Solving this equation for $\bar{t}$, we find

---

[5]By construction, the height function $h(t)$ is *continuous* and *smooth* at all ages. On the other hand, the derivative of the height function $h'(t)$, while continuous, is not smooth at all ages. Instead, $h'(t)$ has a "kink" at age $t = 20$. This has consequences for the rate of change of the volume of the stand. (See footnote 11.)

$$\bar{t}(s) = \left[\frac{a - \sqrt{a^2 - 18b/s}}{2b} \right]^{1/2}. \tag{5}$$

This function is graphed in figure 1. As expected, $\bar{t}(s)$ is a decreasing function of s.

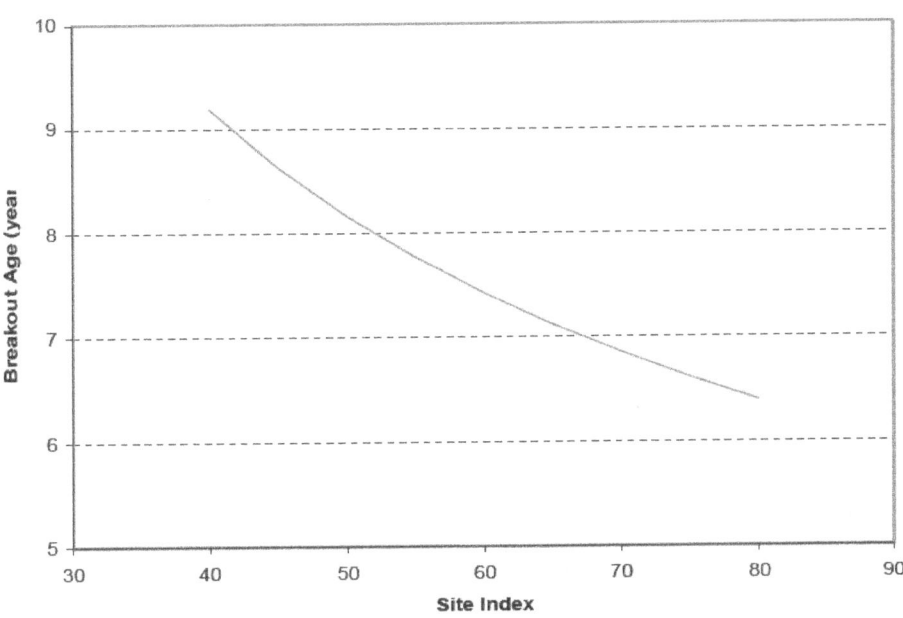

Figure 29 — Breakout age as a function of SI in our model.

The "Basal Area" Model of Basal Area Growth

We frequently use "BA" as an abbreviation for *basal area*. The model described in this section (the BA growth model) and the model described in the following section concern the (gross) basal area growth of a stand. We retain the notation used above, and let $x(t)$ denote the basal area of a stand (in ft^2/acre) at age t. In this notation, the basal area growth rate is given by $x'(t)$, the derivative of $x(t)$ with respect to time. Clearly both $x(t)$ and $x'(t)$ equal zero whenever $t < \bar{t}$.

The BA growth model expresses $x'(t)$ as a function of basal area, age, and site index. The model has 9 parameters $(\beta_0, \beta_1, \ldots, \beta_8)$ and is written as follows:

$$x'(t) = f(x, t, s) = f_0 f_1(x) f_2(t, s) f_3(s) \tag{6}$$

where

$$f_0 = \exp(\beta_0), \tag{6.0}$$

$$f_1(x) = [1 - \exp(-\beta_1 x)]^{\beta_2} \cdot \exp(-\beta_3 x),\tag{6.1}$$

$$f_2(t, s) = \begin{cases} 0 & \text{if } t \leq \bar{t}, \\ \{1 - \exp[-\beta_4(t - \bar{t})]\}^{\beta_5} \cdot \left[t^{-(\beta_6 + \beta_7 s)}\right] & \text{if } t > \bar{t}, \end{cases}\tag{6.2}$$

$$f_3(s) = s^{\beta_8}.\tag{6.3}$$

The purpose for writing the model this way is to separate (as much as possible) the effects on basal area growth attributable to stand density as measured by basal area ($f_1(x)$), age ($f_2(t, s)$), and site index ($f_3(s)$). The estimated values of the parameters are as follows: $\beta_0 = 2.2032$, $\beta_1 = 0.0195$, $\beta_2 = 1.1073$, $\beta_3 = 0.00202$, $\beta_4 = 0.25$, $\beta_5 = 0.5$, $\beta_6 = 0.8102$, $\beta_7 = 0.00193$, and $\beta_8 = 0.7720$. Figures 5, 12, and 13 in the text show the behavior of $f(x, t, s)$ as x, t, and s vary.

Suppose we know $x(t)$, the basal area of a stand at age t, and we want to use eq. (6) to find $x(t + 1)$, the basal area of the stand 1 year later. Equivalently, we wish to find the *change in basal area* between t and $t + 1$, defined as $\Delta x(t) \equiv x(t + 1) - x(t)$. (Note that $x'(t)$ is the *instantaneous* rate of change of basal area, whereas Δx is an *annual* change in basal area.) Equation (6) is a differential equation for $x(t)$, and to find $x(t + 1)$ it's necessary to solve eq. (6) numerically. There are a large number of methods for the numerical solution of differential equations, and there's always a trade-off between *accuracy* and *complexity of implementation*. The method we've chosen is called "the classical fourth-order Runge-Kutta method" and achieves a suitable balance between accuracy and complexity for our model. Let $x = x(t)$. Our approximation of $\Delta x(t)$ is then given by a weighted average of four terms K_1, K_2, K_3, and K_4:

$$\Delta x(t) = \frac{1}{6} \cdot (K_1 + 2K_2 + 2K_3 + K_4)\tag{7}$$

where

$$K_1 = f_0 f_1(x) f_2(t, s) f_3(s),\tag{7.1}$$

$$K_2 = f_0 f_1\left(x + \frac{1}{2}K_1\right) f_2\left(t + \frac{1}{2}, s\right) f_3(s),\tag{7.2}$$

$$K_3 = f_0 f_1\left(x + \frac{1}{2}K_2\right) f_2\left(t + \frac{1}{2}, s\right) f_3(s), \quad \text{and}\tag{7.3}$$

$$K_4 = f_0 f_1(x + K_3) f_2(t + 1, s) f_3(s).\tag{7.4}$$

Although these formulas appear quite complicated, it's straightforward to build them into a computer model.

The "Trees Per Acre" Model of Basal Area Growth

We frequently use "TPA" as an abbreviation for the number of trees per acre. Recall that the BA growth model expresses basal area growth as a function of *basal area*, age, and site index. The BA growth model is the primary engine that drives our simulation of a stand of red pine, but for a variety of reasons we need to augment the BA growth model with a model (the TPA growth model) that expresses basal area growth as a function of *the number of trees per acre*, age, and site index. These reasons may be classified as (1) realism and convenience, and (2) mathematical necessity.

Realism and convenience. From the time of stand establishment until age 20 or 30, TPA is more useful than BA as a quantitative description of stand density (Chapter 3, p. 21-22). It's been found that TPA is a statistically significant predictor of basal area growth in younger stands, but not in older stands. Also, in field practice it's difficult to *measure* BA from the breakout age up through the age of 20 to 30. Instead, in this age range it is common to *infer* BA from TPA, SI, Age, and other data.

Mathematical necessity. Equation (6) is a differential equation for $x(t)$. We know that $x(t) = 0$ for all $t \leq \bar{t}$. From eq. (6.1) it follows that $f_1(0) = 0$. Consequently, one solution of eq. (6) that satisfies the initial conditions is that $x(t) = 0$ for *all* ages t. Obviously, this isn't a very *interesting* solution; we require a solution that allows $x(t) > 0$ for ages t just above the breakout age $\bar{t}$. Under some rather unusual mathematical conditions, eq. (6) may have more than one solution through the singular point $(t, x) = (\bar{t}, 0)$. However, even if eq. (6) satisfies these conditions we have no reason to think that eq. (6) provides a *realistic* description of the dynamics of basal area when $x(t)$ is small, say less than 10 square feet per acre.

In summary, we *need* the TPA growth model to get the simulation "off the ground" (so to speak) at $t = \bar{t}$. Subsequently, as $x(t)$ increases, the BA growth model becomes *more* realistic and the TPA growth model becomes *less* realistic.

We retain all the notation used above, and let n denote the number of stems per acre. The TPA growth model has four parameters $(\gamma_0, \gamma_1, \gamma_2, \gamma_3)$ and is written as follows:

$$x'(t) = g(n, t, s) = \begin{cases} 0 & \text{if } t \leq \bar{t}, \\ \gamma_0 s^{\gamma_1} \{1 - \exp[-\gamma_2 n(t - \bar{t})]\} \cdot t^{-\gamma_3} & \text{if } t > \bar{t}. \end{cases} \tag{8}$$

The estimated values of the parameters of this model are as follows: $\gamma_0 = 26.8434$, $\gamma_1 = 0.3927$, $\gamma_2 = 0.000266$, and $\gamma_3 = 0.9015$. The appearance of $g(n, t, s)$ as a function of n and t is shown in figure 14 in the text.

For ages t just above the breakout age $\bar{t}$, the behavior of $x'(t)$ in the TPA model is determined by the expression in braces on the right-hand side of eq. (8). At these ages, $x'(t)$ is approximately *proportional* to n. As time goes on, however, the behavior of $x'(t)$ is increasingly determined by the term $t^{-\gamma_3}$ furthest on the right, and n has almost no effect on $x'(t)$. Hence, n is an important determinant of basal area growth at ages just above $\bar{t}$, but the importance of n as a determinant of basal area growth diminishes as time increases. This is consistent with observation.

The change in basal area between t and $t+1$ in the TPA growth model is given by the integral

$$\Delta x(t) \equiv \int_t^{t+1} g(n, \tau, s) \, d\tau.$$

If $t+1 \leq \bar{t}$, then $x(t) = x(t+1) = 0$, so $\Delta x(t) = 0$. If $t+1 > \bar{t}$, this integral must be evaluated numerically. Just as there are many methods for the numerical solution of differential equations, there are many methods for the numerical evaluation of integrals, and there's always a trade-off between accuracy and complexity of implementation. Our model uses "Simpson's Rule," described in any text on numerical analysis. If $t < \bar{t} < t+1$ (i.e., at the first time that $t+1$ exceeds the breakout age), Simpson's Rule may be written

$$\Delta x(t) = x(t+1) = \frac{\delta}{3}[4g(n, \bar{t} + \delta, s) + g(n, t+1, s)] \tag{9a}$$

where $\delta \equiv \frac{1}{2}(t+1-\bar{t})$. If $t \geq \bar{t}$, Simpson's Rule becomes

$$\Delta x(t) = \frac{1}{6}\left[g(n, t, s) + 4g(n, t + \frac{1}{2}, s) + g(n, t+1, s) \right]. \tag{9b}$$

Combining the TPA and BA Growth Models

In the simplest version of our simulation, we begin with a newly established stand of red pine with known site index s and given number of trees per acre n. We then proceed to calculate the trajectory over time of the basal area $x(t)$. As noted above, we generally use the TPA growth model to calculate $\Delta x(t)$ for ages t just above the breakout age $\bar{t}$, and use the BA growth model to calculate $\Delta x(t)$ for mature stands. For stands of intermediate age we calculate a "consensus $\Delta x(t)$" by blending the two models in a way that is as seamless as possible.

In more detail, suppose we're given $x(t)$, the basal area of the stand at some age t, and now wish to calculate $x(t+1)$. Let "TPAΔx" denote the value of $\Delta x(t)$ implied by the TPA growth model (as given by eq. (9)) and let "BAΔx" denote the value of $\Delta x(t)$ implied by the BA growth model (as given by eq. (7)). Then consensus $\Delta x(t)$ is calculated as a weighed average of TPAΔx and BAΔx:

$$\Delta x(t) = (1 - w(t)) \cdot \text{TPA}\Delta x + w(t) \cdot \text{BA}\Delta x \tag{10}$$

where $0 \leq w(t) \leq 1$ is an age specific weighing function. Although it's not indicated in the notation, consensus $\Delta x(t)$ generally depends on age t, basal area x, number of trees per acre n, and site index s. We tried a number of functional forms for the weighing function

$w(t)$, none of which resulted in an unqualified success. The rule which yields the most plausible results is a "20 year phase-in rule," defined (recursively) as follows:

> $w(0) \equiv 0$.
> At the *first* age t where $\mathrm{BA}\Delta x > \mathrm{TPA}\Delta x$, $w(t)$ is set equal to 0.05.
> At each of the next 19 years, $w(t)$ is increased by 0.05.
> When $w(t)$ becomes equal to 1, it remains at that value from then on.

This is the rule used in RP2005. It achieves a smooth transition from the TPA model to the BA model over a 20 year period, starting from the age where $\mathrm{BA}\Delta x$ first exceeds $\mathrm{TPA}\Delta x$.

Estimating the Parameters of the BA and TPA Growth Models

Estimation of the parameters of the BA and TPA growth models requires a complex iterative procedure with (at least) four distinct levels.

At the base level, we selected functional forms for the models that are flexible and capable of assuming the shapes required to fit the data. For example, the data clearly show that the basal area growth rate (BAG) increases explosively from zero at the breakout age, quickly reaches a peak, and then drops steadily with age. Consequently, a functional form for $f_2(t, s)$ was selected that is capable of taking this shape. Also, the forms chosen must make biological sense. For example, the functional form of the TPA growth model (eq. (8)) implies that BAG is approximately proportional to n at ages t just above the breakout age $\bar{t}$, but that the influence of n on BAG diminishes to zero as the age of the stand increases.

At the second level, the 4 parameters of the TPA growth model and 7 of the 9 parameters of the BA growth model were estimated by a non-linear least squares procedure[6]. The parameters of the BA growth model were estimated using the full data set of 3,671 observations, and the parameters of the TPA growth model were estimated using 1,058 observations of age 50 or younger.

At the third level, the theoretical (least squares) trajectories of BAG over time for the two models were compared with the data and some "reality checks" applied. For example, the least squares estimates of β_6 and β_7 imply that BAG at high ages (150 to 200 years) in the BA growth model is inversely related to s. That is, the least squares estimates imply that at high ages, stands with the highest site index will have the lowest BAG, and stands with the lowest site index will have the highest BAG. This is unrealistic! To address this kind of

---

[6]The parameters β_4 and β_5 cannot reasonably be estimated from the data. These parameters affect the shape of BAG trajectories at ages t just above the breakout age $\bar{t}$, and there aren't enough observations in the master data set with ages just above $\bar{t}$ to allow these parameters to be estimated reliably. Instead, they were estimated "by eye" by comparison of the implied BAG trajectories with data. In any case, we don't believe that great precision in the estimates of β_4 and β_5 is required, as at these ages consensus Δx is almost certainly determined by the NPA growth model.

difficulty, we reran the non-linear least squares routine while imposing restrictions suitably constructed to eliminate the non-realistic behaviors we'd observed. For example, we found that we could ensure that BAG is an increasing function of s at all ages in the BA growth model by imposing the constraint that $\beta_8 \geq 400\beta_7$.

It is convenient to assess the goodness of fit of a model to data by the "coefficient of determination" R^2. Define SST, the "total sum of squares," to be the sum of the squared deviations of BAG from the overall sample mean. Also, let SSR denote the "sum of squared residuals," where a residual is the difference between an *observed* value of BAG for an observation and the *model* value of BAG. The coefficient of determination is defined as

$$R^2 \equiv 1 - \frac{SSR}{SST}.$$

In a *linear* regression model, R^2 may be interpreted as the proportion of SST that is explained by the model. In a non-linear regression, R^2 cannot be given this precise interpretation. Nonetheless, even in a non-linear model, R^2 is a useful indicator of the goodness of fit of the model to the data. The values of SSR and R^2 obtained from the constrained regressions for the two models are shown below.

	SSR	R^2
BA Growth Model	2,948	0.8534
TPA Growth Model	1,870	0.7702

Also at the third level, the residuals implied by the models were plotted against various variables in a search for "specification errors." If the graph of the residuals against one of the current regressors is not randomly scattered around zero, but shows some systematic variation, the functional form associated with that variable should be adjusted. If the plot of the residuals against a variable that is not currently a regressor shows some significant pattern, that variable should be considered as a potentially useful additional regressor.

Finally, the functional form of $w(t)$ was chosen and the two models were merged in our simulations. If the combined model showed no unrealistic behavior for all possible starting values of n and s, we were done. If not, the two models were incompatible in the sense that under certain circumstances the predictions of the two models were too different to allow a smooth transition from one model to the other. In this unhappy event, it was necessary to go back to an earlier step and make adjustments. This sequence of four steps was repeated until the combined model showed an acceptably low amount of anomalous behavior.

Mortality and Number of Trees Per Acre

Net quantities are obtained when losses due to endemic mortality are subtracted from the *gross* quantities. It's important to make a distinction between *endemic* and *catastrophic* mortality. Catastrophic mortality is mortality caused by events outside of the stand and essentially independent of conditions within the stand; hurricanes and forest fires for example. Endemic mortality is mortality caused by ordinary events within the stand. Endemic mortality is a random process with two components. First, mortality may or may not occur in a stand in a given year, and it cannot be determined in advance which of these two alternatives will happen. Second, if mortality *does* occur in a year, the actual quantity of wood lost to mortality is a *random variable*[7]. The fundamental measure of the quantity of wood lost to mortality is *basal area mortality*, i.e., the square feet per acre of basal area lost to mortality annually. All other quantity measures (e.g., loss of volume per year) are derived from basal area mortality. In particular, the number of trees per acre per year that die and are removed may be derived from annual basal area mortality.

As basal area mortality is a random variable, it has an *expected value* that will generally depend on Age, BA, TPA, SI, and other characteristics of the stand. Let E(BAM) denote expected annual basal area mortality. The average value of annual basal area mortality in our data set is 0.144 ft^2/acre/year. However, E(BAM) varies widely with Age, BA, TPA, and SI.

Our regression model for expected basal area mortality makes use of the identity

$$E(\text{BAM}) = \Pr(\mathcal{M}) \cdot E(\text{BAM} \mid \mathcal{M}) \qquad (11)$$

where $\mathcal{M}$ denotes the event that mortality occurs in a measurement period and $\Pr(\mathcal{M})$ denotes the probability of $\mathcal{M}$. The second term on the right in eq. (11) is a *conditional expectation*: it is the expected value of annual basal area mortality given that some mortality occurs during the measurement period. For our entire data set, $\Pr(\mathcal{M}) = 0.24816$ and $E(\text{BAM} \mid \mathcal{M}) = 0.58054$. (Note that $0.24816 \times 0.58054 = 0.144$, as required by eq. (11).) Models for both $\Pr(\mathcal{M})$ and $E(\text{BAM} \mid \mathcal{M})$ may be estimated from our data.

We first consider $\Pr(\mathcal{M})$. Figure 16 in the text shows the Age and BA of sites with and without mortality. There is a considerable amount of overlap in these two clouds of (Age,BA) coordinates. The only striking difference between these two clouds is that mortality occurred in over 95 percent of the stands with BA over 250 square feet. Also, both Age and TPA appear to be significant explanatory variables for $\Pr(\mathcal{M})$; histograms show that $\Pr(\mathcal{M})$ declines with age after age 50 or so, and $\Pr(\mathcal{M})$ increases with TPA at every age. As there is a strong negative relationship between Age and TPA in our data, the effects of Age, BA, and TPA on $\Pr(\mathcal{M})$ are confounded. A conventional regression model for probabilities is a *logit model*, sometimes called a *logistic regression*. Our logistic regression yields the following:

$$\Pr(\mathcal{M}) = \frac{1}{1 + e^{-y}} \qquad (12)$$

where

---

[7]A "random variable" is a numerical measurement whose value is determined "by chance." For example, the number of heads obtained from 10 flips of a fair coin is a random variable.

$$y = 0.3268 + 0.0189 \cdot \text{BA} - 0.0127 \cdot \text{Age} - 0.0637 \cdot \text{SI} + 0.00112 \cdot \text{TPA}. \tag{13}$$

All of the multiplicative coefficients of eq. (13) are statistically significant at the 0.0001 level. A positive (negative) sign on a multiplicative coefficient indicates that $\Pr(\mathcal{M})$ increases (decreases) with an increase in the associated variable.

Our model for $E(\text{BAM} \mid \mathcal{M})$ was estimated with data from the 907 stands where mortality occurred[8]. Instead of estimating a model for BAM directly, we estimated a model for the "BAM ratio," defined as the ratio of annual basal area mortality to basal area in the stand. The BAM ratio for a stand is the proportion of basal area in the stand lost to mortality per year during an observation period. As the BAM ratio is a proportion, it lies between 0 and 1. Furthermore, as this model was estimated only using stands where mortality occurred, the BAM ratio was always positive. Finally, endemic mortality is never total, so no BAM ratio in our data equaled 1. It is customary to transform a variable known to lie in the interval $(0, 1)$ into a variable that can take any value, and to run the regression on the transformed variable. The usual transform in this situation is the logit transform. Let r denote a BAM ratio. Then the logit transform of r is given by

$$z = \ln\left(\frac{r}{1-r}\right) \quad \text{with inverse transform} \quad r = \frac{1}{1+e^{-z}}.$$

We then ran an ordinary linear regression with z as the dependent variable. This regression yielded

$$z = -4.44458 - 0.02767 \cdot \text{BA} + 0.00008101 \cdot \text{BA}^2 + 0.0000666 \cdot \text{Age}^2. \tag{14}$$

Each of the multiplicative coefficients in eq. (14) are statistically significant at the 0.0001 level. Given z, our estimate for $E(\text{BAM} \mid \mathcal{M})$ may be written

$$E(\text{BAM} \mid \mathcal{M}) = \frac{\text{BA}}{1+e^{-z}}. \tag{15}$$

As above, a positive (negative) sign on a multiplicative coefficient indicates that $E(\text{BAM} \mid \mathcal{M})$ increases (decreases) with an increase in the associated variable.

In summary, we first calculate $\Pr(\mathcal{M})$ with eqs. (12) and (13), then calculate $E(\text{BAM} \mid \mathcal{M})$ with eqs. (14) and (15), and finally calculate $E(\text{BAM})$ with eq. (11). That is,

$$E(\text{BAM}) = \frac{1}{1+e^{-y}} \cdot \frac{\text{BA}}{1+e^{-z}} \tag{16}$$

where y and z are given by eqs. (13) and (14). The appearance of $E(\text{BAM})$ as a function of basal area and age is shown in figure 17 of the text[9].

---

[8]Three stands with "catastrophic" basal area mortality and one stand with an extraordinarily high number of stems were omitted from the data set used to estimate this model.

[9]NOTE. Figure 17 of the text assumes that TPA decreases exponentially over time according to the equation $\text{TPA} = 907.77 \cdot \exp(-0.0186 \cdot \text{Age})$. This equation was derived from a regression of TPA on Age in our master data set.

As mentioned above, all other *net* quantities are derived from basal area mortality. In particular, the expected number of trees that die and are removed per acre per year is derived from $E(\text{BAM})$. Let μ denote the quadratic mean diameter (QMD) at breast height of trees in the stand. A fundamental equation that relates basal area x (in square feet per acre), number of trees per acre n, and QMD (in inches) of trees in a stand at any age is

$$\frac{x}{n} = \frac{\pi\mu^2}{24^2} = \frac{\mu^2}{k} \qquad \text{where} \qquad k \equiv \frac{24^2}{\pi} \approx 183.34649. \tag{17}$$

Equation (17) implies that

$$n = \frac{kx}{\mu^2} \tag{18}$$

and

$$\mu = \left[\frac{kx}{n}\right]^{1/2}. \tag{19}$$

Letting μ_m denote the QMD of trees that die, it follows from eq. (18) that the expected number of trees per acre per year that die and are removed is given by

$$\Delta n = k \cdot \frac{E(\text{BAM})}{\mu_m^2}. \tag{20}$$

It's a commonplace observation that the average diameter of trees that die is less than the average diameter of trees in the stand. We assume (somewhat arbitrarily) that μ_m is one standard deviation below μ. More precisely, we assume that

$$\mu_m = \max\{\mu - \sigma, 1\} \tag{21}$$

where σ denotes the standard deviation of DBH in the stand. Our estimate of σ as a function of μ is given by[10]

$$\sigma = \sigma(\mu) \equiv \lambda(t-1)\left(\frac{2.9723 \cdot \mu}{7.7734 + \mu}\right). \tag{22}$$

The quantity $\lambda(t-1)$ is a "deflationary factor" included because thinning from either above or below has the effect of narrowing the distribution of DBH in the residual stand. This is explained in the section on thinning below. (Prior to any thinning λ is initialized to 1.) Note that $\sigma(\mu)$ is an *increasing* function of μ.

---

[10]This formula is used only in years where no thinning takes place. The formula for the calculation of the

Volume, Volume Change, and Board Feet

From $x(t)$, $n(t)$, and $h(t)$, one may derive the volume of wood in a stand and several other important quantities. The volume of wood (in ft^3/acre) in a stand of red pine of age t is given by

$$V(t) = 0.4085\,(1 - R)x(t)h(t) \tag{23}$$

where R is a "yield reduction factor," $x(t)$ is the basal area and $h(t)$ is the height of the stand at age t. Hence, the change in volume between ages t and $t+1$ is given by $\Delta V(t) = V(t+1) - V(t)$. This change can be either *gross* or *net*; see the following section.

For some purposes, it's interesting to examine the instantaneous rate of change of volume, given by the derivative $V'(t)$, as a function of age and basal area. From eq. (23) it follows that

$$V'(t) = 0.4085(1 - R)[x(t)h'(t) + h(t)x'(t)] \tag{24}$$

where $x'(t)$ is given by the BA growth model [eq. (6)] and eq. (3) implies that

$$h'(t) = \begin{cases} \alpha s\gamma(1 - e^{-\beta t})^{\gamma-1} \cdot \beta e^{-\beta t} & \text{for} \quad t \geq 20, \\ s(2at - 4bt^3) & \text{for} \quad 0 \leq t \leq 20. \end{cases} \tag{25}$$

The behavior of $V'(t)$ as a function of Age, BA, and SI is illustrated in figure 6 of the text[11].

An alternative measure of volume is the number of *board feet* of merchantable timber in the stand at any time. Our calculation of board feet from $x(t)$, $n(t)$, and $h(t)$ is somewhat complicated and requires some additional assumptions. From eq. (19) it follows that the QMD of trees in the stand is given by

$$\mu = \left[\frac{kx(t)}{n(t)}\right]^{1/2}.$$

Let σ denote the standard deviation of DBH of trees in the stand. We now *assume* that DBH is distributed *normally* with mean μ and standard deviation σ. This assumption allows us to compute the number of trees per acre that are in any particular diameter class. "Board feet" is only defined for trees whose diameter exceeds some critical amount (set by the user), say d_{crit}. Let d be an integer between 7 and 45, inclusive. By "DBH class d," we mean the set of trees whose DBH satisfies $d \leq \text{DBH} < d + 1$. The number of board feet of wood per acre in the stand is then given by the sum

---

[11]Recall from footnote 1 of this appendix that $h'(t)$ in our model has a "kink" at age $t = 20$. This has the unfortunate (but unavoidable) consequence that $V'(t)$ also has a kink at age 20.

$$\text{Total BF} = \sum_{d=d_\text{crit}}^{45} (\text{BF in DBH class } d).$$

The number of board feet in DBH class d is given by the product of 4 quantities:

$$\text{BF in DBH class } d = \left(\frac{\text{BF}}{\text{CF}}\right)_d \times \left(\frac{\text{MV}}{\text{TV}}\right)_d \times \text{NT}(d) \times \text{VMT}(d)$$

where $(\text{BF/CF})_d$ denotes the ratio of board feet to cubic feet in DBH class d, $(\text{MV/TV})_d$ denotes the ratio of merchantible volume to total volume in DBH class d, $\text{NT}(d)$ denotes the number of trees in DBH class d, and $\text{VMT}(d)$ denotes the cubic foot volume of the median tree in DBH class d. We obtained tables of $(\text{BF/CF})_d$ and $(\text{MV/TV})_d$ for red pine in the Lake States from Mark Hansen of the North Central Research Station (see text footnote 3). The number of trees in DBH class d is given by

$$\text{NT}(d) = n(t)\Big[F(d+1\,|\,\mu,\sigma) - F(d\,|\,\mu,\sigma)\Big]$$

where $F(\,\cdot\,|\,\mu,\sigma)$ denotes the cumulative distribution function (cdf) of a normal random variable with mean μ and standard deviation σ. Finally, $\text{VMT}(d)$ is given by

$$\text{VMT}(d) = 0.4085\,(1-R)\cdot\text{BAMT}(d)\cdot h(t)$$

where $\text{BAMT}(d)$ denotes the basal area (in square feet) of the median tree in DBH class d, and is given (approximately) by

$$\text{BAMT}(d) = \frac{1}{k}\left(d + \frac{1}{2}\right)^2 \approx 0.005454154\left(d + \frac{1}{2}\right)^2.$$

(See eq. (17)). Assembling these pieces, we find that

$$\text{BF}(t) = (1-R)n(t)h(t)\sum_{d=7}^{45} c_d[F(d+1|\mu,\sigma) - F(d|\mu,\sigma)] \qquad (26)$$

where

$$c_d \equiv I(d \geq d_\text{crit}) \times \left(\frac{\text{BF}}{\text{CF}}\right)_d \times \left(\frac{\text{MV}}{\text{TV}}\right)_d \times 0.4085 \times \frac{1}{k}\left(d + \frac{1}{2}\right)^2$$

$$I(d \geq d_\text{crit}) \equiv \begin{cases} 1 & \text{if} \quad d \geq d_\text{crit}, \\ 0 & \text{if} \quad d < d_\text{crit}, \end{cases}$$

$F(\,\cdot\,|\mu,\sigma) \equiv$ the cdf of a normal r.v. with mean μ and standard deviation σ,

$\mu =$ the QMD of the stand at age t, and

$\sigma =$ the standard deviation of DBH in the stand at age t.

Although this procedure seems logical, and the numbers it produces seem reasonable, one should keep in mind that the procedure hinges on a long string of assumptions, many of which are plausible at best. Users of RP2005 are therefore advised to regard its predictions about board feet as rough estimates rather than as precise predictions. Our computation should be considered a *theoretical maximum* of board foot volume in the stand.

Stand Dynamics: Overall Framework

We have modeled growth and yield of red pine as a discrete time dynamic model. The variable t representing the age of the stand in years takes integral values from 0 to 200. At the beginning of year t we know the basal area per acre $x(t)$, the height $h(t)$, and the number of trees per acre $n(t)$. From these quantities we may calculate volume (measured both in cubic feet and in board feet), the QMD of trees in the stand, and other variables of interest. The models described above are combined with a model of thinning in order to compute $x(t+1)$, $n(t+1)$, the value of BA and TPA at the beginning of the following year.

In any year that thinning takes place, we assume that thinning *precedes* growth and mortality. This seems realistic enough, as thinning operations generally take place while trees are dormant. On the other hand, it's a somewhat arbitrary modeling decision whether thinning is to precede or follow growth and mortality, as every dormant period both follows and precedes a period of growth and mortality.

It's important to understand the modeling consequences of the decision to let thinning precede growth and mortality. Consider a period where thinning occurs, and suppose at the beginning of the period we have basal area x and number of trees n. (We're omitting the argument t for simplicity.) Following thinning, the stand has a reduced basal area x' and a reduced TPA n'. During the remainder of the period the stand experiences some growth and mortality. Note that this subsequent growth and mortality depend on x' and n', the *post-thinning* basal area and TPA, and not on x and n.

Stand Dynamics: Thinning

RP2005 allows the user to specify a thinning regime in a very flexible way. The user may choose up to 20 stand ages at which thinning may occur. At each age where thinning is allowed, the user then specifies a "target value" for basal area to remain on the site after thinning, and a "d/D ratio" that describes how the size of trees removed during thinning differs from the size of trees that remain on the site.

In order to describe this specification precisely, it's necessary to introduce some notation. Consider an age where thinning may occur, and let x and n denote the basal area and number of trees per acre at the beginning of the period. From eq. (19) we know that the quadratic mean diameter of trees in the stand is given by

$$\mu = \left[\frac{kx}{n}\right]^{1/2} \qquad \text{where} \qquad k \equiv \frac{24^2}{\pi} \approx 183.34649.$$

Now let the subscript 1 label quantities associated with *thinned* trees, and let the subscript 2 label quantities associated with *residual* trees, i.e., trees left standing on the site after thinning is completed. In this notation, x_1 is the basal area of trees removed by thinning, x_2 is the "target" value of basal area, n_1 is the number of trees removed by thinning, and n_2 is the number of trees that remain on the site following thinning. (If $x \leq x_2$, no thinning takes place.) Clearly,

$$x_1 + x_2 = x \qquad \text{and} \qquad n_1 + n_2 = n.$$

From these quantities we may calculate the QMD of both thinned and residual trees:

$$\mu_1 = \left[\frac{kx_1}{n_1}\right]^{1/2} \qquad \text{and} \qquad \mu_2 = \left[\frac{kx_2}{n_2}\right]^{1/2}. \tag{27}$$

The "d/D ratio" is defined as the ratio of the QMD of trees removed to the QMD of trees that remain on the site after thinning. Using the notation introduced here, the d/D ratio r is defined as $r \equiv \mu_1/\mu_2$. If $r < 1$, trees that are removed are smaller on average than trees that remain, and we have "thinning from below". Conversely, if $r > 1$ we have "thinning from above". As we are given both x and x_2, it follows that $x_1 = x - x_2$. The computation of n_1 and n_2, however, is not obvious. It may be shown that[12]

$$n_1 = n\left(\frac{x_1}{x_1 + r^2 x_2}\right). \tag{28}$$

We then calculate $n_2 = n - n_1$. All other statistics of thinned and residual trees (except board feet) may be derived from x_1, n_1, x_2, and n_2.

Let σ_1 and σ_2 denote the standard deviation of DBH of the harvested trees and in the residual stand, respectively. We need to know σ_1 and σ_2 in order to calculate board feet contained in the harvested trees and in the residual stand. Also, we need to know σ_2 in order to calculate the number of trees that are expected to die per year in the residual stand. If the stand is thinned from below, it follows that $\mu_1 < \mu < \mu_2$, while if it is thinned from above, then $\mu_2 < \mu < \mu_1$. Let σ denote the standard deviation of DBH in the pre-thinned stand. If σ, σ_1, and σ_2 are all calculated by the use of eq. (22), it follows that we would have

$$\sigma_1 < \sigma < \sigma_2$$

if the stand is thinned from below, or

$$\sigma_2 < \sigma < \sigma_1$$

if the stand is thinned from above. These inequalities are implausible. Whether the stand is thinned from above or below, we expect to find that

[12]The reader may confirm eq. (28) by showing that it implies that μ_1/μ_2 is equal to r.

$$\max\{\sigma_1, \sigma_2\} < \sigma.$$

That is, if the stand is partitioned into two subsets and DBH is used as a criterion for which subset a tree goes into, then we expect each subset to have a narrower distribution of DBH than the pre-thinned stand. Hence, eq. (22) doesn't provide us with a plausible method for calculating σ_1 and σ_2 whenever $r \neq 1$. To proceed we need to make an assumption about the relative size of σ_1 and σ_2. We assume that $\sigma_1 = \sigma_2$. That is, we assume that the variance of DBH is equal in the two subsets. Under this assumption, it may be shown[13] that

$$\sigma_1 = \sigma_2 = \sqrt{\sigma^2 - \frac{n_1 n_2}{n^2}(\mu_1 - \mu_2)^2}. \tag{29}$$

This formula is used to calculate σ_1 and σ_2.

For any values of $x, n, x_2 < x$, and the d/D ratio r, eq. (28) yields a legitimate value for n_1. Then $x_1 = x - x_2$ and $n_2 = n - n_1$ are legitimate values for x_1 and n_2, and eq. (27) yields legitimate values for μ_1 and μ_2. However, the same conclusion does not extend to eq. (29). If $r = 1$ there's no problem, as $\mu_1 = \mu_2 = \mu$ and $\sigma_1 = \sigma_2 = \sigma$ in this case. But if r differs too much from 1, then it may happen that

$$\sigma^2 - \frac{n_1 n_2}{n^2}(\mu_1 - \mu_2)^2 < 0,$$

which implies that σ_1 and σ_2 are *imaginary* numbers! Hence, if this condition occurs at a thinning, the d/D ratio specified by the user is actually *impossible* given the conditions of the stand at the moment it is to be thinned. In this event, the simulation halts and an error message is printed. The user must adjust the d/D ratio specified for this thinning to something closer to 1, and d/D ratios at subsequent thinnings may also require adjustment.

If eq. (29) is used to compute the standard deviation of DBH in the residual stand, but eq. (22) is used without adjustment to compute the standard deviation of DBH in the stand in the years following thinning, then an unrealistic jump in this standard deviation will occur. To avoid this, we need to adjust the deflationary factor λ as follows. If thinning takes place in year t, then $\lambda(t)$ is set equal to

$$\lambda(t) = \sigma_2 \left(\frac{7.7734 + \mu_2}{2.9723 \cdot \mu_2} \right). \tag{30}$$

In subsequent years (until the next year when thinning occurs), $\lambda(t)$ slowly (at a rate of 2.5 percent per year) returns to 1 according to the equation

$$\lambda(t+1) = 1 - 0.975[1 - \lambda(t)].$$

---

[13]Without going into the details, this follows from a well known identity of probability theory: for any two random variables X and Y,

$$\mathrm{Var}(Y) = \mathrm{E}[\mathrm{Var}(Y|X)] + \mathrm{Var}[\mathrm{E}(Y|X)].$$

Stand Dynamics: Growth and Mortality

The mathematical models developed in the preceding sections may be combined into a specification of the dynamics of a stand of red pine. It's convenient to consider separately the simulation of a stand grown from age 0 (from seed) and the simulation of an already established stand.

First consider a stand grown from age 0. We begin with a plot of bare ground with a known site index s and a number of established trees per acre $n(0)$. We initialize the weight function $w(0)$ to 0. We wish to use our models to calculate the conditions of the stand at ages $t = 1, 2, 3, \ldots$. The computations proceed recursively. That is, given "input" values $x(t)$, $n(t)$, etc. at age t, we may calculate the "output" values $x(t + 1), n(t + 1)$, etc. In any year where thinning takes place, the input values are the values of BA and TPA *after* thinning has taken place, but before any growth or mortality has occurred.

This calculation takes place in four stages. In the first stage, eq. (10) is used to calculate $\Delta x(t)$, the consensus change in basal area for the year from t to $t + 1$. This is the *gross* change in basal area; that is, this calculation does not include any loss of basal area due to mortality. In the second stage, therefore, the expected annual amount of basal area lost to mortality is calculated, say

$$\text{EBAM}(t) \equiv E(\text{BAM}) \tag{31}$$

where $E(\text{BAM})$ is given by eq. (16). In the third stage we use eqs. (19), (22), (21), and (20) to calculate Δn, the expected number of trees lost to mortality and removed during this year. Finally, we combine these results to obtain $x(t + 1)$ and $n(t + 1)$:

$$x(t + 1) = x(t) + \Delta x(t) - \text{EBAM}(t) \tag{32}$$

and

$$n(t + 1) = n(t) - \Delta n. \tag{33}$$

Please note that the quantity

$$\Delta x(t) - \text{EBAM}(t) \tag{34}$$

on the right-hand side of eq. (32) denotes the *periodic annual increment* (PAI) of basal area between ages t and $t + 1$. The expected net cubic foot volume of the stand at time $t + 1$ is given by

$$V(t + 1) = 0.4085 \, (1 - R)x(t + 1)h(t + 1)$$

and the expected net increase in volume over the period is given by $V(t + 1) - V(t)$.

The quantities $x(t)$ and $V(t)$ are *net* basal area and *net* volume at age t. We're also interested in the dynamics of *gross* basal area and *gross* volume of the stand. Roughly, gross BA at some age t is the basal area that the stand would have *if* no basal area had been lost to mortality since some arbitrary starting age $t_0 < t$. Gross basal area at age t_0, denoted

$\text{GBA}(t_0)$, is defined as $x(t_0)$, the net basal area of the stand (after thinning if the stand was thinned) at age t_0. The gross basal area of the stand for all ages $t > t_0$ is calculated recursively by

$$\text{GBA}(t+1) = \text{GBA}(t) + \Delta x(t) \tag{35}$$

where $\Delta x(t)$ is the gross change in basal area during the year[14]. From eqs. (32) and (35), it follows that

$$\text{GBA}(t) - x(t) = \sum_{\tau=t_0}^{t-1} \text{EBAM}(\tau). \tag{36}$$

That is, gross basal area at age t differs from net basal area at age t by the amount of expected basal area mortality accumulated since t_0. Gross volume at age t is given by

$$\text{GV}(t) = 0.4085\,(1-R)\cdot\text{GBA}(t)\cdot h(t),$$

so the annual change in gross volume is given by

$$\text{Gross } \Delta V = \text{GV}(t+1) - \text{GV}(t).$$

This completes our description of the dynamics of a stand grown from age 0, and we now consider the simulation of an existing stand. RP2005 provides for the needs of the owner or manager of an existing stand who wishes to anticipate the consequences of alternative possible management regimes. The purpose of the remainder of this section is to describe how the stand dynamics must be modified in this case.

The initial basal area of a stand grown from age 0 is necessarily zero, but if the age of an existing stand is greater than the breakout age $\bar{t}$ the basal area of the stand will be positive. For stands with age between $\bar{t}$ and 30, however, it might be impossible or inconvenient to measure this basal area with any great precision. We've equipped RP2005 with a means for the user to either provide, or to decline to provide, an initial basal area. The stand dynamics differ somewhat in these two cases.

Suppose, then, that the user has a stand of known age t_0, site index s, and initial number of trees per acre $n(t_0)$, and wishes to simulate this stand into the future. As t_0 is the age of the stand at the moment the user wishes the simulation to begin, we call t_0 the "initial" age of the stand. Also, the user may, or may not, have a measurement of initial basal area $x(t_0)$.

If the user chooses to provide RP2005 with $x(t_0)$, the simulation proceeds into the future (i.e., at ages $t_0 + 1, t_0 + 2, \ldots$) exactly as described as above except that the weighing function $w(.)$ is initialized to zero at age t_0 instead of at age zero.

The situation is slightly more complicated if the user chooses not to provide RP2005 with an initial value of basal area. In this case, RP2005 begins with a preliminary simulation.

---

[14]Note that $\Delta x(t)$, the change in *gross* basal area, depends on $x(t)$, the *net* basal area, and on $n(t)$, the *expected* number of trees per acre.

A stand of red pine with site index s and initial number of trees per acre $n(t_0)$ is simulated from age 0 to age t_0, suppressing all mortality. These calculations yield a stand of age t_0 with the correct number of trees per acre $n(t_0)$, an estimated value of the basal area $x(t_0)$, and an estimated value of the weighing function $w(t_0)$. This preliminary simulation is invisible to the user and yields no output statistics. Upon completion of the preliminary simulation, the simulation proceeds into the future (i.e., ages $t_0 + 1$, $t_0 + 2, \dots$) exactly as described above.

Instantaneous Rates of Change

Figures 10, 11, and 12 of RP2005 show the periodic annual increment (PAI) and the mean annual increment (MAI) of basal area, volume, and board feet. There's a small amount of ambiguity in the description "periodic annual increment," and the first purpose of this section is to describe precisely what is shown in these graphs. (There's no ambiguity in the meaning of MAI.) The graphs labeled PAI actually show *instantaneous rates of change* of these variables, rather than changes that take place annually. The "annual increment" of a variable is actually an *average* of the instantaneous rate of change of that variable over the course of a year. For example, consider $x(t)$, the basal area of the stand at age t. The instantaneous rate of change of basal area is given by $x'(t)$, while an "annual increment" of basal area is

$$x(t+1) - x(t) = \int_t^{t+1} x'(\tau) \, d\tau.$$

The advantage of graphing instantaneous rates of change is that we may thereby show the instantaneous effects of thinning on these rates of change.

The second purpose of this section is to explain how these instantaneous rates of change are calculated.

The instantaneous rate of change of *gross* basal area is a function of age t, basal area x, number of trees per acre n, and site index s, and is given by

$$\text{Gross BAG} = (1 - w(t))g(n, t, s) + w(t)f(x, t, s)$$

where $g(n, t, s)$ is given by eq. (8) and $f(x, t, s)$ is given by eq. (6). To obtain the instantaneous rate of change of *net* basal area, we need to subtract Δn, the expected number of trees that die per year, from Gross BAG. That is,

$$x'(t) \approx (1 - w(t))g(n, t, s) + w(t)f(x, t, s) - \Delta n. \tag{37}$$

From eq. (20),

$$\Delta n = k \cdot \frac{E(\text{BAM})}{\mu_m^2}, \tag{20}$$

where

$\mu_m \equiv \max\{\mu - \sigma, 1\},$

$\mu \equiv$ the QMD of the stand $= \sqrt{kx/n},$

$\sigma \equiv$ the standard deviation of DBH in the stand,

$E(\text{BAM}) = \dfrac{1}{1 + e^{-y}} \cdot \dfrac{x}{1 + e^{-z}},$

$y = 0.3268 + 0.0189x - 0.0127t - 0.0637s + 0.00112n,$

$z = -4.44458 - 0.02767x + 0.00008101x^2 + 0.0000666t^2.$

Both basal area x and TPA n change "instantaneously" when the stand is thinned. These changes immediately affect μ, μ_m, y, z, $E(\text{BAM})$, Δn, $g(n, t, s)$, and $f(x, t, s)$, and consequently have an immediate effect on $x'(t)$. This will appear as a vertical segment at age t in a graph of $x'(t)$.

Now consider the effect of thinning on $V'(t)$, the instantaneous rate of change of cubic foot volume. From eq. (23) it follows that

$$V'(t) = 0.4085(1 - R)[x(t)h'(t) + h(t)x'(t)] \tag{24}$$

where $x'(t)$ is given by eq. (37). Neither $h(t)$ nor $h'(t)$ is affected by thinning operations, but both $x(t)$ and $x'(t)$ are. Hence, at any age t where thinning occurs, the graph of $V'(t)$ will display a vertical segment.

Finally, we consider the effects of thinning on $\text{BF}'(t)$, the rate of change of board feet with respect to age. From eq. (26), we have

$$\text{BF}(t) = (1 - R)n(t)h(t)S_1(t) \tag{38}$$

where $S_1(t)$ denotes the sum

$$S_1(t) \equiv \sum_{d=7}^{45} c_d[F(d + 1 | \mu, \sigma) - F(d | \mu, \sigma)]. \tag{39}$$

It follows that

$$\text{BF}'(t) = (1 - R)[n'(t)h(t)S_1(t) + n(t)h'(t)S_1(t) + n(t)h(t)S_1'(t)]. \tag{40}$$

Now $n'(t) \approx -\Delta n$ where Δn is given by eq. (20), and $h'(t)$ is given by eq. (25). All that remains is to find $S_1'(t)$. This requires a fair amount of tedious algebra. We first define a function $\phi(.)$ as follows: for any real number z,

$$\phi(z) \equiv \frac{1}{\sqrt{2\pi}} \exp\left(-\frac{z^2}{2}\right).$$

(The reader might recognize this as the probability density function of a standard normal random variable.) Next, for each $d \in \{7, 8, \ldots, 45\}$, we define

$$z_d \equiv \frac{d - \mu}{\sigma}$$

where μ is the QMD of the stand and σ is the standard deviation of DBH in the stand. It may be shown that

$$S_1'(t) = \frac{1}{\sigma} \left[\frac{d\mu}{dt} S_3(t) + \frac{d\sigma}{dt} S_4(t) \right] \qquad (41)$$

where

$$S_3(t) \equiv \sum_{d=7}^{45} c_d [\phi(z_d) - \phi(z_{d+1})],$$

$$S_4(t) \equiv \sum_{d=7}^{45} c_d [z_d \phi(z_d) - z_{d+1} \phi(z_{d+1})],$$

$$\frac{d\mu}{dt} = \frac{1}{2} \mu \left[\frac{x'(t)}{x(t)} - \frac{n'(t)}{n(t)} \right],$$

and

$$\frac{d\sigma}{dt} = \frac{0.0743075\mu[1 - \lambda(t-1)]}{7.7734 + \mu} + \frac{24.1049\lambda(t-1)}{(7.7734 + \mu)^2} \frac{d\mu}{dt}.$$

In RP2005, the sums $S_1(t)$, $S_3(t)$, and $S_4(t)$ are computed in the worksheet "DBH Class Sums." This worksheet also contains another sum, $S_2(t)$, defined as

$$S_2(t) \equiv \sum_{d=7}^{45} \widehat{c}_d [F(d+1|\mu,\sigma) - F(d|\mu,\sigma)] \qquad (42)$$

where

$$\widehat{c}_d \equiv I(d \geq d_{\text{crit}}) \times 0.4085 \times \frac{1}{k} \left(d + \frac{1}{2} \right)^2. \qquad (43)$$

This sum may be used to compute the cubic foot volume of sawtimber:

$$\text{CF Volume of Sawtimber} = (1 - R)n(t)h(t)S_2(t). \qquad (44)$$

Appendix IV. Definition of Terms

Metric Equivalents

When you know:	Multiply by	To find
Number/acre	2.471	Number/hectare
Inches (in)	2.540	Centimeters (cm)
Feet (ft)	0.3048	Meters (m)
Yards (yds)	0.9144	Meters (m)
U.S. statute miles (mi)	1.6093	Kilometers (km)
Square inches(in^2)	6.4516	Square centimeters (cm^2)
Square feet (ft^2)	0.0929	Square meters (m^2)
Acres (ac)	0.4047	Hectares (ha)
Square miles (mi^2)	2.5899	Square kilometers (km^2)
Square feet/acre (ft^2/ac)	0.2296	Square meters/ha (m^2/ha)
Cubic feet (ft^3)	0.0283	Cubic meters (m^3)
Cubic feet/acre (ft^3/ac)	0.06997	Cubic meters/hectare (m^3/ha)
Standard cord (128 ft^3)	3.6220	Cubic meters (m^3)
1,000 board feet (MBF Int 1/4)	~6.4 (small trees) ~4.3 (large trees)	Cubic meters (m^3)

Glossary

BA = Basal area (ft^2/acre)

d.b.h. = Diameter Breast Height at 4.5 feet, in inches outside bark.

MAI = Mean Annual Increment

MBF = 1,000 board feet (International 1/4 rule)

PAI = Periodic Annual Increment

QMD = Quadratic Mean Diameter (Diameter of tree of mean BA)

SI = Site index (Dominant stand height at age 50 from seed)

Stand Age = Age from seed

TPA = Number of trees/acre

Scientific Names of Trees and Shrubs

Common name	Scientific name
Red Pine	*Pinus resinosa*
Eastern white pine	*P. strobus*
Jack pine	*P. banksiana*
Loblolly pine	*P. taeda*
Slash pine	*P. elliottii*
Ponderosa pine	*P. ponderosa*
Southern pines	*Pinus* spp.
Balsam fir	*Abies balsamea*
Douglas fir	*Pseudotsuga menziesii*
White spruce	*Picea glauca*
Cedar	*Thuja* spp.
Maples	*Acer* spp.
Birches	*Betula* spp.
Oaks	*Quercus* spp.
Elms	*Ulmus* spp.
Aspens	*Populus* spp.
Poplars and cottonwoods	*Populus* spp.
Willow	*Salix* spp.
Hazel	*Corylus* spp.
Dogwood	*Cornus* spp.
Alder	*Alnus* spp.